Psychology and Organizations

Michael Coates

Heinemann

Heinemann Educational Publishers
Halley Court, Jordan Hill, Oxford, OX2 8EJ
a division of Reed Educational and Professional Publishing Ltd

OXFORD MELBOURNE AUCKLAND
JOHANNESBURG BLANTYRE GABORONE
IBADAN PORTSMOUTH (NH) USA CHICAGO

Heinemann is a registered trademark of Reed Educational and Professional Publishing Ltd

Text © Michael Coates, 2001

First published in 2001

05 04 03 02 01
10 9 8 7 6 5 4 3 2 1

302.35
COA

3 wte Main

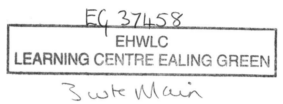

British Library Cataloguing in Publication Data
A catalogue record for this book is available from the British Library

ISBN 0 435 80657 2

1 3 APR 2010

Typeset by Wyvern 21 Ltd
Picture research by Thelma Gilbert
Printed and bound in Great Britain by The Bath Press Ltd, Bath

Acknowledgements

The publishers would like to thank the following for permission to reproduce copyright material: *Administrative Science Quarterly* for 'Median Correlations between LPC scores and group performance measures obtained in original and validation studies (only)'. Vol. 17, No. 4, Fig. 1, on p. 61. Reprinted from 'The Effects of leadership training and experience: a contingency model interpretation' by FE Fiedler, published by *Administrative Science Quarterly*, December, 455. By permission of *Administrative Science Quarterly*; *Harvard Business Review* for 'The five components of emotional intelligence at work' from 'What Makes a Leader' by Daniel Goleman, November–December 1998 on p. 21; for 'How the hygiene motivator factors affect job attitudes in six countries' and 'Principles of vertical job loading (job enrichment)' from 'One More Time: How do you motivate employees?' by Frederick Herzberg, September–October 1987 on pp. 39 and 40. Copyright © 1998 and 1987 by the President and Fellows of Harvard College; all rights reserved; Knight Features for the Dilbert cartoons on p. 29; News International Limited for the article on p. 39, © Times Newspapers Limited (2000); Pearson Education for Figure 3.8 on p. 65 © P.W. Betts, 2000. Reprinted by permission of Pearson Education Limited.

Cover photograph by AKG London

The publishers would like to thank the following for permission to use photographs: Empics/Adam Davy, p. 72; Hulton Getty, pp. 46 and 60; Photofusion, pp. 37 and 53; Popperfoto, p. 18; Popperfoto/Reuters, p. 26; the Science Photo Library/NASA, p. 75; Steven Wiltshire, p. 10.

The publishers have made every effort to contact copyright holders. However, if any material has been incorrectly acknowledged, the publishers would be pleased to correct this at the earliest opportunity

Tel: 01865 888058 www.heinemann.co.uk

C Contents

1 Introduction

Since ancient times when slaves were motivated through fear of death, there has been an active interest in how to get the best out of workers. Studying people at work is a mixture of sociology, management and psychology, with occupational psychology having more recently developed a status of its own. This book reflects the range of disciplines involved in the study of people at work but concentrates on the use of psychology.

The book considers the process of recruiting, paying, motivating, managing and appraising employees, before discussing how increasingly people are working not as individuals but as part of a team. The latest psychological influences (some would say pseudo psychology) are included, for instance emotional and spiritual intelligence along with neuro linguistic programming.

Chapter 1

This chapter examines the recruitment process. Firstly, it details the process by which this is achieved, before looking at three main topics: intelligence testing, personality questionnaires and interview technique. Readers will gain a thorough understanding of the principles behind these processes and realize why they are controversial and often not effective.

Chapter 2

Here we take the new employee and show how he or she would be motivated and rewarded. Then we look at how stress is an increasing part of working life, as is redundancy and early retirement.

Chapter 3

The desire for more effective management has generated a whole industry of consultants, trainers and academic awards. This chapter can only touch on this vast subject, explaining the main theories of leadership with an emphasis on communication, one of the key methods for improving the effectiveness of employees.

Chapter 4

Increasingly, people do not work as individuals with one boss, but in teams with many bosses (or no boss at all). This chapter provides a comprehensive background to why this has happened and how teams form, change and avoid conflict.

How to use this book

This book has a number of features to help you understand the topic more easily. It is written to give you a wide range of skills in preparation for any of the new AS and A level psychology syllabi. Below is a list of the features with a brief summary to explain how to use them.

1 Real Life Applications

These consist of 'text boxes' which develop further a concept already discussed within the main text. Often they provide articles or outlines of studies. In all cases they attempt to apply theory to real life situations.

2 Commentary

These paragraphs appear throughout the book. They follow on from issues raised within the main text. They serve a number of functions: to provide an evaluation of the earlier text, to clarify a point or to highlight some related issue. Sometimes they provide 'for' and 'against' debates.

3 Key studies

These are descriptions of important studies within a specific area. There are two of these in each chapter. They briefly identify the aims, method, results and conclusions of the study. This feature helps you understand the methodology of research.

4 Questions

Each 'Real Life Application' has two or three short answer questions, designed to test a range of skills including: summarizing, outlining and evaluating. All of these activities are designed to allow you to acquire the study skills outlined within the syllabi.

In addition, two or three 'essay style' questions are included at the end of each chapter. They relate specifically to the material covered within that chapter.

5 Advice on answering questions

At the end of the book there is a short section that gives advice on answering the essay and short answer questions presented in the book.

1 Recruitment

This chapter details the recruitment process and concentrates on some of the techniques that have a higher emphasis on psychology, for instance intelligence and personality testing. Real Life Applications that are considered are:

- RLA 1: Lives blighted by high IQ
- RLA2: American Express uses emotional intelligence.

What is an organization?

An organization is a collection of people who interact and work towards a common goal and whose relationships to each other are determined by a laid-down arrangement or structure.

Organizations could be companies, charities, voluntary groups or sports teams. In this book, we will be talking primarily about companies, i.e. where people work, but on the whole, the theories covered apply in all organizations.

There are many schools of thought concerning how to look at organizations, including **Scientific Management** and the **Human Relations School**. They differ in that those who subscribe to the scientific approach, such as FW Taylor, would look at laying down *how* organizations *should* work. Human relations advocates such as Elton Mayo (see p. 43) would look at how people react in certain situations and from this consider how to make the organization run more effectively. More recently, in his book *Images of organisations*, Gareth Morgan (1998) looked at organizations from eight different viewpoints. According to Morgan, organizations can be regarded as being like:

- machines
- organisms
- brains
- cultures
- political systems
- psychic prisons
- flux and transformation
- instruments of domination.

The way in which individuals think about an organization will influence the way they will suggest it should be made more effective and will in turn influence the way they feel managers should motivate, organize and lead their people.

Organization structure

Organizations have a structure, for instance a school, with its governors, head teacher, deputy head, key stage leaders and teachers. Alternatively, it could be a project team where the person in charge of the project is not the manager of those on the project team.

A traditional hierarchical (layered) structure is shown in Figure 1.1. Because there are lines going up between people these are called 'line' relationships

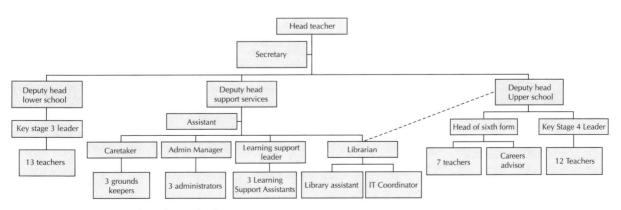

Figure 1.1: Organization chart for a school

such as 'line manager'. If people have some authority over others, but only when they are dealing with certain aspects of their job (e.g. the finance manager has the final say on any aspects of finance, whoever does it), these are called 'dotted line' relationships.

More recently, there has been considerable emphasis on flattening organizations by taking out levels of management and empowering people lower down to make decisions that previously their manager had to make. In this situation people often have to lead projects and 'manage' people, even though they are not officially managers and the others do not have to do what they ask. These are called **matrix structures** and are discussed on p. 59.

For many years managers and theorists have looked at making organizations more effective. Often, on the news you will hear that a company has 'reorganized', which means that it has altered the structure, probably requiring less people to do the same work. Examples would be the banking industry which, through new technology, now requires far fewer people than it did before. As use of this technology progressed, for instance using debit cards rather than cheques, those departments that worked in the old way would get smaller and eventually disappear, leaving the organization with a new structure.

Human resources

Employees are often referred to as human resources. This phrase is controversial as some would say that it ranks employees alongside machines and software in how they are regarded by management. The analogy is based on the fact that like machines, or software, organizations want employees who are cost effective and work hard, with the minimum of trouble.

The process for recruiting employees is similar to that of buying equipment, apart from the fact that it is far more difficult to 'return' an employee who doesn't turn out to be as good as expected!

Recruitment process

The recruitment process is shown in Figure 1.2.

Job analysis

Assuming that an employee leaves and his or her work cannot be reorganized, or job sharing utilized, then a new employee needs to be recruited. The first step, once authorization to recruit has been given, is to complete a job analysis.

A job analysis is a:

'systematic analysis of activities, resources, inputs, outputs and behavioural aspects of a job role.'

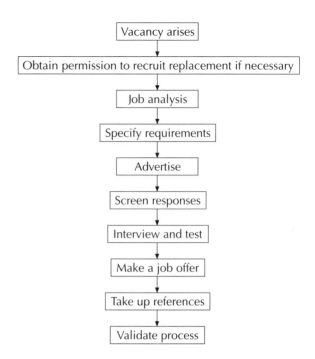

Figure 1.2: Recruitment process

It is used for:

- writing job descriptions
- job classification
- job evaluation
- job design
- training needs analysis
- building person specifications
- performance appraisal
- worker mobility studies
- efficiency studies
- safety
- manpower planning
- legal requirements (Ash and Levine, 1980).

It can be **job orientated** covering the processes, equipment, inputs and outputs of a job and/or **person orientated**, covering the behavioural and psychological aspects of the role. To complete a job analysis, information is required about the job and the jobholder's skills.

Job analysis – sources of information

Direct observation

This involves following, possibly videoing, the current job-holder at work.

Job-holder analysis

Job-holder analysis is useful and is the most common method. It involves the current job-holder writing down exactly what he or she does and what skills are required.

Flannagan (1954) developed **critical incident technique**, a procedure which involves the job-holder detailing specific incidents of behaviour that either aid effective work or are a hindrance. For instance:

'The most common event on a Monday is a customer returning goods they bought on Saturday. They are often very annoyed that the goods are faulty or simply frustrated that they had to leave work to return them. You need to be very patient and keep calm. You must word your questions in such a way so that they do not think you are criticizing them. You can often solve their problem if you ask the right questions. Often they really do not know what they want so you have to ask lots of questions and really get to the core of the problem. The customers often leave very happy, even if they have had to spend more money, if they end up getting what they really needed.'

From this statement the following skills appear to be critical:

- patience
- subtle questioning
- emotional resilience
- questioning technique.

Commentary

Critical incident technique allows the interviewer to build up a bank of key skills required for a job and with the help of the job-holder, his or her colleagues and manager, these skills can be divided into essential, preferred and optional. The division is necessary, otherwise the perfect human would be required to fill the role.

These critical skills are also called **behaviours** or **competencies**. In this book, the term competencies will be used.

Position analysis questionnaire (PAQ)

Developed by McCormicke *et al* in 1972, the PAQ comprises approximately 200 questions covering six areas:

- information input
- mental processes used
- work outputs
- interpersonal actions
- work context/situation
- other aspects of work.

Commentary

As with a number of the techniques that now exist, the PAQ is limited by the fairly high degree of reading and verbal reasoning skills required by the user (Ash and Edgell, 1975).

The PAQ and its derivatives are often used to compare and contrast the views of the job-holder and his or her manager concerning the competencies required for a job role. On the whole, studies have shown a reasonable correlation (link) between the two people's views of the job. However, Friedman and Harvey (1986) also found a high correlation between PAQ questionnaires completed by the job-holder and 'naïve raters' such as students, who were simply going by what it says in the job description and making assumptions about the required competencies.

Selecting the correct method

McCormick developed the PAQ around competencies displayed by American workers, and the cross-cultural differences apparent in business behaviour limits its use outside of the USA. In 1983, Barts *et al* developed the **job component inventory** (JCI) which focuses on both the aspects of the job and the behaviours required, then attempts to quantify the level of skill required for each aspect. The JCI was developed within the field of education and has rarely been used elsewhere. When selecting a job analysis method it is vital to find out if it was based on a comparable occupational sector to the one in question.

Repitory grid

Another popular but often-misunderstood procedure for job analysis, is the **repitory grid** (Kelly, 1955).

It is used with managers who are asked to differentiate between three individuals who work for them. They highlight competencies that one has, that makes them more effective than the others, thereby building up a competency model for that role. The particular benefit of this technique is that it involves the line managers and asks them in a structured way to consider the qualities of actual people who have performed the job in the past (Newcombe and Bywater, 1999).

The following is an example of a repitory grid from SHL *Guidelines for Best Practice*:

'Jane and Jean prepare by reading and planning before divisional meetings. Peter relies on thinking on his feet and his contributions are usually not as useful.'

POSITION PROFILE
Marketing Communications Manager

Main Purpose of the Position (including reporting structure)

To generate a high profile, high quality image for the organization to major Original Equipment Manufacturers and end users in the truck, bus, construction, marine, rail, defence and agricultural industries.

Key Responsibilities: (Must include relevant responsibility for quality as per Cummins Quality Policy)

Producing customer magazines.
Press release writing and distribution
Development of the UK web site
Producing promotional materials to support the sales and marketing teams for both ongoing work and new product launches.
Exhibition booking, design and organization.
Maintaining all processes to ensure that Cummins quality procedures are adhered to.
Ensuring that all marketing activities reflect the ethical standards of Cummins.

Experience Required:

Proven experience of marketing communications in a business to business environment (preferably manufacturing). Must have excellent copy writing and PC skills.

Education/qualifications required (classify as essential and optional):

Preferably a degree and ideally a CIM qualification

Most Critical Skills:

<u>Functional/Technical</u>	<u>Quality/Improvement</u>	<u>Teamwork</u>	<u>Leadership</u>
Copy writing	Attention to detail	Relationship building	Strategic thinking
Exhibition design	Data analysis	Communication skills	Understanding customer needs
PC skills		Managing disagreements	

Approved by:	Date:	Position Holder:	Date:

© Cummins inc.

Figure 1.3: Position profile

Peer assessment

Typically, using a structured questionnaire or inter-view, work colleagues are asked to detail the job's content and skill requirements from their point of view. This may highlight certain requirements for team cohesion, such as they must be able to cope with tight deadlines and be able to work overtime at short notice.

Documentation

Documents such as job descriptions, training manu-als, inputs (e.g. an order form), outputs (e.g. an invoice) help to build up a picture of the role and the skills required.

Job description

Once the job analysis is complete a job description can be created. Typically, it will cover the following points:

- job title
- who the role reports to
- broad description of role
- key responsibilities
- identification of main customers
- method in which effectiveness will be measured.

Person specification

Following on from the job description, the **person specification** identifies the characteristics of the ideal job-holder. Traditionally, this included factors such as physical characteristics, education, training and personality, but nowadays specifications are written in terms of competencies.

Job or position profile

Combining both the job description and the person specification, the job or position profile allows the recruiter to see at a glance the role and requirements (see Figure 1.3).

Job advert

Once the job profile is complete, the information gathered can be used to create both an internal advert to go on company notice boards or the Intranet and an external advert to go in vacancy sec-tions of printed media and/or on the Internet.

The rules for creating a job advert are similar to those used for creating a product advert (see Figure 1.5) and can be remembered by the acronym AIDA: Attention, Interest, Desire, Action.

Part of a prestigious, international organization, Cummins Engine Co in the UK consists of a number of highly successful businesses, operating at the forefront of technology, working across global markets.

Leaders in the fields of diesel engine manufacture, power generation, turbocharger and ac generator technologies, we've created a world class business, whose key product markets are in the automotive, off highway and industrial sectors.

Here in New Malden, our Publicity Unit provides a company-wide service, supporting UK and European operations in the Central Area, taking in Africa and the Middle East.

We are an Equal Opportunities Employer, striving to improve diversity in our workforce. We actively encourage applications from all minority groups.

© Cummins inc.

c.£30,000 + Car + Bonus Opportunities   **New Malden, Surrey**

MARKETING COMMUNICATIONS MANAGER

Spreading The Corporate Message – Business to Business

As Marketing Communications Manager, working closely with a wide variety of internal customers and external suppliers, your brief will be to generate a high profile, high quality image for the organisation with major OEM's and end users in the truck/bus, construction, marine, rail, defence and agricultural industries.

Driven by corporate, marketing and distributor demands, you'll enjoy plenty of creative input, taking responsibility for the production of customer magazines, press releases, web based material, marketing and promotional work, as well as organizing exhibitions and events on an international basis.

Degree qualified and ideally from an engineering or industrial marketing background, you must have extensive marketing communications experience, on a business to business basis, linked to proven design, copywriting and PC skills. In addition, we also expect the ability to absorb technical details and deliver quality work to tight deadlines.

Interested? Then please send full CV and salary details, quoting ref NM3, to: xxxxxx xxxxxxx xxxx xxx xxxxx x xxxxx xxxxxx xxxxxx xxxxx xxxx xxxxxxxxx xxx xxxx xxxxxx xxxxx x xxxxxxxx

Unfortunately, we are unable to respond to all applications, however, if shortlisted for interview, we will contact you within 4 weeks.

Visit our website: www.cummins.com

For graduate trainee/placement opportunities, go to www.activatecareers.co.uk and quick search Cummins

No agencies please.   *Closing Date: Monday 24th July 2000.*

Figure 1.4: Adverts should reflect the details shown in a position profile

Attention

The advert must stand out from those competing for the space and potential applicants.

Interest

It must be written in such a way that potential employees want to read on and find out more.

Desire

If possible, the advert should create the desire to apply.

Action

The advert should encourage and make it easy to apply. Adverts should not be too cramped or 'wordy' and should sell the company and the role, without over inflating the attributes of either. A better match between those who apply and the person required will be obtained if the wording states the requirements explicitly and indicates who would and who would not be suitable. Inserting a salary range also helps candidates identify whether the role is for them.

Application screening

Following 'publication' of the advert, candidates will either send for an application form or, more commonly, will send in a CV and a covering letter, or apply online. Whatever the method of application, the recruiter will find that many of the applications are not suitable and must screen out those that should not be considered.

Using the information on the position profile the recruiter should look for evidence in the CV. It is generally only possible to do this for quantifiable skills such as specific qualifications, languages or software skills. 'Soft' skills such as 'communication skills' are very difficult to see in a CV and statements such as 'possessing excellent communication skills' should not be taken as evidence!

Internet recruiting allows screening to be done automatically, as certain responses cause the software to allocate points to the application and eventually all applications are ranked in points order. Assuming that the screening criteria were set fairly, computerized screening is more effective at avoiding bias (see p. 18).

Selection methods

Once a shortlist of candidates has been identified, the recruiter must select the most appropriate selection technique. Figure 1.5 shows the main tech-

niques and their **validity**. Validity in this instance is the *predictive ability of the selection method to choose someone who at subsequent appraisal will be found to be fully effective.*

Validity is explained in more detail on p. 16. For now, it is sufficient to know that a perfect prediction would have a validity of 1. Anything over 0.4 would be regarded as a good predictor; however, the higher, the better.

A combination of the above recruitment methods will gain a higher validity as shown by assessment centres which contain multiple selection methods.

Psychometric tests

To screen out shortlisted candidates, psychometric tests are often used. A **psychometric test** is 'a stan-dardized sample of behaviour' that can be described by a numerical scale or category system (Cronbach, 1984.) These consist of three main forms:

- intelligence tests
- ability or aptitude tests
- personality questionnaires.

Many organizations rely very heavily on these techniques. For instance, the computer giant Microsoft values intelligence over most other attributes, while many service industries value specific personality attributes.

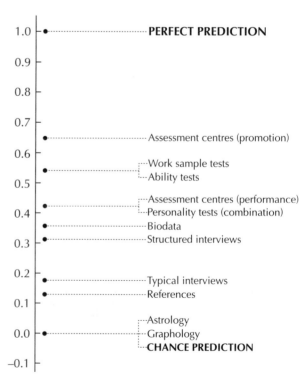

Figure 1.5 Validity of various recruitment methods

Commentary

As both intelligence and personality are regularly assessed as a means to identify the best candidate, it is essential that those involved in the process have a good understanding of both and should wherever possible be qualified to administer and interpret tests. Qualifications are issued by the British Psychological Society at Level A ('intelligence'/ability testing) and Level B (personality questionnaires).

With that in mind, the next section goes on to detail the theories of intelligence and personality and about how they can be assessed.

What is intelligence?

Intelligence is difficult to define as opinions vary as to whether it is:

- a **concept** that we can use to explain why some people do well at certain activities,
- an **inherent cognitive ability** – something that's simply there, like speech or hearing
- the **level of intellectual performance** that someone achieves at any point in time
- an **ascribed quality** – something that others think you have.

Commentary

It is easy to reify intelligence. Reification is to view a concept as if it is an actual thing that objectively exists.

Definitions of intelligence

- Sternberg and Salter (1982) view intelligence as:

'A person's ability for goal directed adaptive behaviour'.

- Calvin (1998) states:

'…to most observers, the essence of intelligence is cleverness, a versatility in solving novel problems'.

- Phares (1997) summarizes the most common definitions in one statement:

'Intelligence is the ability to adapt to a variety of situations both old and new; an ability to learn or the capacity for education broadly conceived and an ability to employ abstract concepts and to use a wide range of symbols and concepts.'

- Boring (1923) defined intelligence as:

'What intelligence tests measure'.

This definition isn't as weak as it first appears, because, if intelligence can't be defined in itself, then if someone undertakes a range of cognitive tests, it stands to reason that *intelligence must be what they are assessing.*

Is intelligence one or several abilities?

Charles Spearman (1923) analysed correlation studies showing people who had done well in maths and English tests. This led him to propose that the correlation between doing well in both tests indicates that humans have an underlying level of intelligence that will lead people to score similar results across a range of tests.

Spearman called this underlying intelligence 'G'. The differences that were apparent between tests he proposed were due to factors specific to certain tests or 'S'. Despite recognizing the existence of specific test factors (S), Spearman emphasized the **unitary nature of intelligence**, i.e. that intelligence is an actual and single characteristic of a person.

Thurstone

Thurstone (1938) disagreed with Spearman's two-factor (G and S) theory of intelligence, believing that a better explanation was to look at **seven primary mental abilities** that together make up intelligence:

- verbal comprehension
- verbal fluency
- inductive reasoning
- spatial visualization
- number skills
- memory
- perceptual speed.

Commentary

At the end of his career though, Thurstone wrote that these seven factors correlated, i.e. that on average those who do well in one test are indeed likely to do well in the others, thereby supporting Spearman's theory of G after all.

Guilford

Guilford (1967) also developed a model of intelligence that focused on a combination of specific abilities (see Figure 1.6).

Guilford maintained that 150 abilities could be assessed independent of each other – a **differential model of intelligence**. This differential approach, especially when combined with job analysis (p. 2), has led to the creation of aptitude or ability tests for employment selection.

Guilford like Spearman and Thurstone also eventually accepted a correlation between contents,

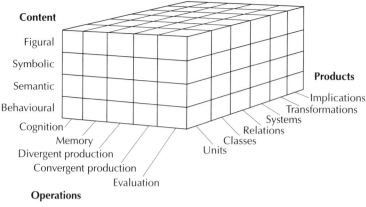

Figure 1.6: Guilford's model of intellect, SHL Group PLC

operations and products, thus supporting the notion of G (that people have one intelligence).

Gardner

Gardner (1983) maintains that intelligence cannot be measured with paper and pencil tests as there is no single thing called intelligence (i.e. that G doesn't exist). This is based on the fact that the:

'tests rule out intelligent acts such as giving an impromptu speech or finding your way around a strange town.'

Gardner feels that any valid theory of intelligence must incorporate studies of:

- gifted individuals
- Savants (see p. 10)
- neuropsychology
- experts and virtuosos
- diverse cultures.

Gardner's model has eight completely independent 'intelligencies':

1 **Linguistic** – e.g. Polish author Joseph Conrad learned English as a sailor, yet went on to write classics of English literature.
2 **Spatial** – comprehending shapes and images in three dimensions, a feature of the right side of the brain. This intelligence allows us to navigate, sculpt and identify objects by touch.
3 **Interpersonal intelligence** – the ability to interact and understand others.
4 **Intrapersonal intelligence** – the ability to understand and sense our self as displayed by self-esteem or strength of character. Autistic people often lack this.
5 **Naturalistic intelligence** – the ability to identify and classify patterns in nature. Originally, this would have been used to identify edible plants.

6 **Musical** – the ability to comprehend, perform and compose music with ease.
7 **Bodily kinesthetic** – a natural sense of how your body should act or react in demanding situations. Sometimes develops in children before other intelligencies, and is apparent in many sports champions.
8 **Logical mathematical intelligence** – an ability to mentally process logical problems and equations.

Other differential models

Vernon proposed a hierarchical model of intelligence in tests of 1000 World War II recruits, with a battery of tests (see Figure 1.7).

Testing 'intelligencies'

General intelligence tests have long existed in the UK, e.g. the 11+ used to select which form of secondary education can be pursued.

Alfred Binet and Theodore Simon looked at testing intelligence as a means of identifying children who would benefit from remedial education. They maintained that intelligence could be measured by assessing the child's ability to answer questions. By testing many children, it was possible to show answers that a typical child of a certain age should be able to

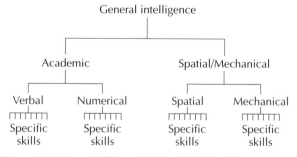

Figure 1.7: Vernon's hierarchical model of intelligence

Sternberg

answer (norm table) (see Key Study 1). Once a test is complete it is possible to compare the results with answers expected for each age and state the 'mental age' of that child.

KEY STUDY 1

Researchers:	Binet and Theodore (1904)
Aims:	To respond to the French Minister for Education's concerns that children with behavioural problems were receiving less education by more effective identification of such children.
Method:	Using a set of standardized tests, hundreds of Parisian school children were tested so as to form a norm table consisting of average scores for each age group. Subsequent testing of children allowed comparison with those norm tables, thereby showing whether their mental age (as indicated by their expected score) was the same as their actual age.
Results:	Clear differences in abilities were shown for each age although the researchers did not attempt to reason why scores varied nor whether 'intelligence' develops at a uniform rate with age.
Conclusions:	That less-bright children should be identified and given mental exercises to develop their attention span and self discipline.

Measuring intelligence

Binet had simply wanted to identify learners who were behind those of the same age, whereas **Galton** had wanted to find a method of quantifying 'G' or overall intelligence. An advocate of Galton's work was **Lewis Terman** (1877–1956) who adapted Binet's tests for American students by adding further tests, creating American norm tables to compare results with and extending the use of such tests to adults. Reflecting the university at which he worked, these tests became known as the **Stanford Binet tests** and in various forms are still used today.

German psychologist **William Stern** came up

with an effective way of using these test results to calculate a measurement of comparative intelligence, the **Intelligence Quotient** or **IQ**. The IQ was originally a person's mental age (as identified by Binet's tests) divided by their actual age (multiplied by 100 to remove any decimal point).

Thus:

$$IQ = \frac{\text{Mental age}}{\text{Chronological age}} \times 100.$$

Commentary

An average child whose mental and actual age is the same will have an IQ of 100, whereas a 6-year-old with the mental age of a 10-year-old would have an IQ of 125.

This calculation is less useful for adults, for instance if a 30-year-old tests as well as a 20-year-old, does he or she really only have an IQ of 66, or if you reverse the ages, an IQ of 150?

Today, IQ relates to someone's ability compared to a representative large sample of people called a norm group. 100 is still the average, with most people falling between 85 and 115. The phrase IQ is still used but it is no longer a true 'quotient', simply a result of the test.

Intelligence – an emotive subject

Intelligence is not only a complex and highly researched subject but also an emotive one.

Commentary

Can we actually measure intelligence? If intelligence, or more specifically IQ, is all important in assessing people's ability to undertake certain jobs, enter mainstream education or enrol in certain universities, then we need to understand it better and ensure that tests are fair.

Examples of where 'IQ' doesn't seem right

Ceci (1986) argues that many aspects of intelligence are not reflected by IQ scores, as outlined below.

Brazilian street children

Many Brazilian street children are capable of doing the maths required for their survival even though they failed mathematics at school (Carrater and Schleiman, 1985).

Women shoppers in California

Many had no difficulty in comparing product values at a supermarket but were unable to do the same mathematical operations in paper and pencil tests (Lave, 1988).

Gamblers

In a study of expertise in wagering on horses, Ceci and Liker (1986) found that skilled handicappers naturally use a highly complex interactive model with as many as seven variables. The ability to do this successfully was unrelated to scores on intelligence tests.

Flynn (1987) studied IQ results in the Netherlands. In 1952 only 0.38 per cent had an IQ over 140 (genius). Yet in 1982, scored by the same norms, 9.12 per cent exceeded that figure. Flynn concluded that these gains could not be real, and it must be that 'abstract problem solving' ability had improved or some other factor was at play. Flynn also feels that the IQ measure is only a weak correlate of real intelligence, if such a thing exists (see RLA 1).

Real Life Application 1:

Lives blighted by high IQ

Fifty years ago, Jonathon Cocking from Middlesex was dubbed 'the Child Wonder' when he appeared in the newspapers at the age of three. He read the newspapers each day, could count to a million and recite Shakespeare. When the reporter arrived, the toddler stated, 'I am three and three quarter years, I weigh 3 st 2lb. I am 3 ft 8 ins, quite tall for my age don't you think?'. When he started primary school his IQ was 150. However, by the time he took his A levels he had lost interest in academic studies and got three average grades before going on to fail the first year of a BSc in chemistry.

Now he works making personalized number plates from a workshop in his garden. Jonathon feels now that being labelled a child prodigy was a disadvantage and 'in any event IQ tests really show little more than the ability to do IQ tests'. He believed that being told he was gifted, gave him confidence but made him think, quite wrongly, that life would be a pushover.

Jonathon has four children of his own plus a stepdaughter. The eldest is a member of Mensa and is unemployed. The other two natural children are excelling at school as is his stepdaughter, which Jonathon believes shows that the way children are brought up has a vital part to play in how intelligent they are.

Article adapted from 'Lives blighted',
Daily Mail, 8 July 2000.

Summary

- Jonathon Cocking was a 'child genius'. However, he did not succeed academically.
- All of his children including a stepdaughter appear to be intelligent, thereby indicating that the environment is just as much a factor in intelligence as genetics.

Questions

1 What are the main criticisms of measuring IQ?

2 What factors could explain his stepdaughter's high intelligence?

Savant Syndrome

Savant ('foolish wise one') Syndrome is where mentally impaired individuals display amazing mental talents. Savant Syndrome is widely known through the intricate drawings of Stephen Wiltshire, who as a teenager was able to produce intricate drawings of scenes after just one viewing, despite being autistic.

Drawing by Stephen Wiltshire who has Savant Syndrome

The film *Mercury Rising* starring Bruce Willis revolved around an autistic boy who was able to see words written in the world's most hard-to-decipher code – he was a Savant.

Genetics or heritability of intelligence

In any group of people, both environmental factors and genetic factors play a part in explaining differences in IQ among the members. Genes are passed down or inherited from parents; the influence of this on any characteristic of the child is called '**heritability**'.

Any figures quoted for heritability apply to groups not to individuals, as the environment and testing errors could have had a significant influence on *that individual*. For a *large group*, however, it may be possible to ascertain that a certain percentage was inherited. It is also a relative index and it will change over time and between groups as their circumstances alter; it is a snapshot figure for that group. Heritability when shown as a number is referred to as h^2, the **heritability coefficient.**

Heritability and the individual

While heritability studies apply to groups, the study of twins would appear to offer an opportunity to examine the impact on individuals. Unfortunately, studies of twins continue to be affected by the similarity of their upbringing and environment. Twins reared apart are difficult to find and inevitably their environments vary. Despite the difficulty in completing such studies, there is evidence that genetically related individuals display greater similarity in their measured intelligence.

Table 1.1 shows that there is a stronger correlation

Table 1.1: Difference in correlation between intelligence of genetically linked individuals

Genetic relationships	Developmental status	Median correlation
Unrelated persons	Reared apart	.01
Unrelated persons	Reared together	.23
Foster-parent-child	Living together	.20
Parent-child	Living together	.50
Siblings	Reared apart	.40
Siblings	Reared together	.49
Dizygotic twins	Reared together	.53
Monozygotic twins	Reared apart	.75
Monozygotic twins	Reared together	.87

Reprinted with permission from 'Genetics and Intelligence: A Review' by L. Erlenmeyer-Kimling and L. F. Jarvik, *Science*, December 1963, Vol. 142, p. 1478. Copyright 1963 the American Association for the Advancement of Science.

(link between two factors) for monozygotic (identical) twins reared together and their measured level of intelligence, than for instance the intelligence levels of two people sitting next to each other on the bus (unrelated people).

The foster parent/child correlation of 0.2 is also far higher than for unrelated individuals, thus indicating the influence of environment. Horn (1983) found a correlation of 0.28 between the IQ of adopted children and their biological parents and only 0.15 with their adopted parents, i.e. the hereditary link appears stronger. On the other hand, Horn *et al* in 1979 identified families where there were adopted and natural children. The correlation between the mother's IQ and both types of children was virtually identical.

Studies by Cyril Burt and later the 'Minnesota study of twins reared apart', found that on average 77 per cent of intelligence is influenced by genes (h^2= 0.77) and 23 per cent their environment.

Group differences

Individual differences in hereditary intelligence are therefore difficult to prove, with most evidence relating to groups, as mentioned above. This fact has caused intense debate, particularly when a book called *The bell curve* by Hernstein and Murray (1994) was published (see Key Study 2).

KEY STUDY 2

Researchers:	Hernstein and Murray (1994)
Aims:	To collate and interpret the results of studies on intelligence published in the USA since the mid-1970s.
Method:	To conduct a meta analylsis of published work on intelligence and to track the results of aptitude tests undertaken by 12 686 American students aged in 1979 between 14 and 22 over a 12-year period. The tests were made more broad ranging in 1980 as the US military wanted to use the norm tables to assess potential recruits.
Results:	552 pages of findings with 280 pages of appendices, which claimed to reveal a dramatic transformation in American

	society, with it becoming increasingly divided between those who are intelligent and those who are not. In addition, considerable evidence was gained showing the relative intelligence of different ethnic groups.
Conclusions:	The book claimed to reveal a dramatic transformation in American society with it becoming increasingly divided between those who are intelligent and those who are not. The inference could be taken from this that policy makers (i.e. the government) should either discourage the use of testing and other measures for intelligence or discourage less intelligent groups from having more children.

The bell curve

So controversial that it was not shown to critics prior to publication, *The bell curve* has brought about public debate in the USA. Hernstein and Murray argue that individuals have always differed in intelligence, partly because of hereditary factors but these differences matter more now due to the importance society puts on people achieving success. Those with high IQs achieve positions of power and those with low IQs are kept down in low-paid jobs. The authors emphasize the links between low intelligence and criminals, the unemployed and illegitimate children and their parents.

The authors allude to the notion that it is inevitable that if we regularly test intelligence and segregate society (through jobs, universities, etc.) a them and us situation will develop in the population – the 'them' being the impoverished, criminal and less intelligent and the 'us' being the rich intelligent. The implication could be taken as being that policy makers already try to influence birth rates so they should discourage such groups having children. This would herald a return to the **eugenics** style of American birth control policies.

The bell curve also reinforced research that shows the average IQ of white Americans is around 8 points higher than that of black Americans regardless of socio-economic status.

Commentary

Hernstein and Murray correctly point out a number of differences in intelligence between ethnic groups. It is the 'spin' they put on it that has caused so much upset. For instance:

'An immigrant population with low cognitive ability will again on average have trouble not only finding good work but have trouble in school, at home and with the law.'

East Asians, whether they live in America or Asia, do score on average higher than caucasians on intelligence tests. Similarly, European Americans on average score higher than African Americans.

Correlation does not, of course, explain the differences. However, it is easy for individuals to conclude from this that white people are more intelligent than black people and therefore intelligence tests by their very nature discriminate against black people and should not be used for employment selection. This ill-informed viewpoint resulted in intelligence tests no longer being allowed in a number of US states to assess candidates for job selection.

Response to The bell curve

In response to *The bell curve*, the American Psychological Society produced a report called 'Intelligence known and unknown' (1996). The report concluded that:

'Intelligence tests particularly predict individual differences in school achievement. In this respect the skills measured are important. However, achievement levels (overall grades) can also vary depending upon teaching style and hours taught.

Test scores also correlate with measures of accomplishment e.g. adult occupational status, but to an extent this is inevitable, as such tests are used to allow students entry to certain courses required for specific professions.

Differences in genetic endowment (hereditary) contribute substantially to differences in psychometric test results but the way in which genes produce their effects is unknown.

The environmental factors contribute substantially to the development of intelligence but it is not clear what those factors are or how they work.

Role of nutrition remains unclear.

The differential between mean intelligence scores of Blacks and Whites does not result from any obvious biases in test construction and administration, nor does it simply reflect differences in socio-economic status. There is no support for a genetic interpretation. At this time no one knows what is responsible.

Although there are no important sex differences in overall intelligence test scores, substantial differences do appear for specific abilities. Males score higher on visual, spatial and mathematical skills, while females excel on verbal measures. Sex hormone levels are closely related to some of these differences but social factors presumably play a role as well.'

Is intelligence culturally defined?

Some psychologists maintain that intelligent behaviour varies with the situation, for instance Binet and others think of intelligence relating to how well people cope with academic work. Similarly, in western society for many prestige jobs it might mean excellent social skills; for street children it might mean being 'street smart'; and for a nomad, it might mean the ability to find water. If intelligence is not culturally defined then it should be possible to swap those people listed above and find they can cope equally well in their new surroundings!

Why test intelligence for job selection?

There is evidence to show that 'G' assessed by a broad range of tests does predict employee performance in job training (i.e. how effectively an employee will take on board new skills). Rees and Earles studied air force personnel who had participated in 89 different job training programmes. They found a very high correlation (0.76) between 'G' and training performance, whether they were hard or easy courses.

Behling (1998) proposes the model illustrated in Figure 1.8 to show the relationship between general intelligence and job performance.

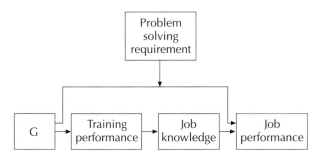

Figure 1.8: Behling's model of how intelligence affects job performance

Republished with permission of the Academy of Management from the *Academy of Management Executive*, Vol. 12, no. 1, pp. 77–87, January 1998; permission conveyed through Copyright Clearance Center, Inc.

Schmidt *et al* (1992) also found a high correlation between intelligence and performance when a new job is being learned. They also found that the relationship between intelligence and performance is most strong for supervisors and above.

Rees studied intelligence and job performance in the air force and concluded that, at supervisory level upwards, the correlation was so strong (0.44) that:

'if an employer were to use intelligence tests only and select the highest scoring applicant for each job, overall the performance from the employees selected would be maximized'.

Otgan (1994) and Behling (1998) indicate that a combination of intelligence and 'Conscientiousness' (assessed by personality questionnaires) increases the predictive element of testing. Behling proposed a model for deciding whether to concentrate more on testing intelligence and conscientiousness or to rely primarily on precisely matching candidates with the position profile (see Table 1.2).

Table 1.2: Behling's model

Rely primarily on g and conscientiousness when …	Rely primarily on precise matching when …
The new employee will be called on to do a great deal of problem solving.	The new employee will be called on to do little or no problem solving.
The new employee will have a high degree of autonomy, i.e. he or she will work pretty much on his or her own.	The new employee will be closely monitored or performance problems will be otherwise obvious to his or her superior.
The skills and abilities the new employee will learn on the job are more important than those he or she brings to the job.	The skills and abilities that the new employee brings to the job are more important than the things he or she will learn on the job.
The new employee must learn the job rapidly and adapt equally rapidly to job changes.	The new employee will have plenty of time to learn the job and can expect to deal with few, gradual changes, if any.
Two or more top job candidates are practically equal in terms of key skills and abilities.	One job candidate is clearly superior to the others in terms of key skills and abilities.

Commentary

Evidence from validity tests of modern ability tests shows they are good predictors if the abilities tested closely reflect those required for the job.

Unfortunately, it is still very common for employers to use the same tests whatever the job.

Exam results

Assuming that there is a link between intelligence and job performance, then surely employers could just go by the applicant's qualifications. Qualifications, however, are not tests of intelligence, they are awards for completing a course and remembering and applying enough material in an exam (for which you only need to get approximately 40 per cent right). Personal circumstances might mean that exams could not be taken or higher education afforded. For these reasons recruitment for the British Armed Forces involves achieving good results on intelligence tests rather than having certain qualifications. With so many A level students now getting top grades, top universities are finding it difficult to make fair selections, and are starting to consider the use of additional intelligence tests.

Ability or aptitude tests

While controversy exists over intelligence tests (measuring G), the testing of specific abilities (or intelligencies) required for a job is a common method of deciding upon the best candidate. Ideally, candidates would be asked to display these abilities by doing the job itself, but this is rarely possible. In practical roles such as hairdressing however, it is standard practice for candidates to:

- show certificates of training
- show photographs of hairstyles that they have done.
- bring a friend and cut and style the individual's hair in front of the employer.

While such an approach is impractical for many roles, particularly ones that involve cognitive rather than manual abilities, it is possible to simulate some skills. For instance, at United Technologies, which makes the wiring for cars, in a series of exercises candidates coil, bend and crimp wires. They are timed and the quality is checked. This manual dexterity test is very similar to the work they would be doing.

In customer contact situations it is common for candidates to role play handling a customer, and there are many commercially produced simulations for this type of industry. In call centres, telephone skills are assessed at interview and often the interview is held over the telephone.

Modern ability tests

Used in occupational selection modern ability tests tend to be grouped under eight headings, comparable with the various multiple intelligence models detailed on p. 8.

Verbal Test

In this test, you are given two passages, each of which is followed by several statements. Your task is to evaluate the statements in the light of the information or opinions contained in the passage and to select your answer according to the rules given below.

MARK CIRCLE A
if the statement is patently **TRUE** or follows logically, **given the information or opinions contained in the passage**

MARK CIRCLE B
if the statement is patently **UNTRUE** or the opposite follows logically, **given the information or opinions contained in the passage**

MARK CIRCLE C
if you **CANNOT SAY** whether the statement is true or untrue or follows logically **without further information**

> The big economic difference between nuclear and fossil-fuelled power stations is that nuclear reactors are more expensive to build and decommission, but cheaper to run. So disputes over the relative efficiency of the two systems revolve not just around the prices of coal and uranium today and tomorrow, but also around the way in which future income should be compared with current income.

1. The main difference between nuclear and fossil-fuelled power stations is an economic one.

2. The price of coal is not relevant to discussions about the relative efficiency of nuclear reactors.

3. If nuclear reactors were cheaper to build and decommission than fossil-fuelled power stations, they would definitely have the economic advantage.

Figure 1.9: Example of verbal reasoning test, SHL Group PLC

1 Verbal

Includes spelling and grammar tests for clerical staff. Verbal reasoning tests, which assess the ability to make logical conclusions from written information, are used at more senior levels. Verbal application tests assess vocabulary and understanding (see Figure 1.9).

2 Numerical

Depending upon the job's need for numerical skills, the test can cover either simple arithmetic or the ability to read information for statistical tables and solve business calculations (see Figure 1.10).

3 Diagrammatic

These tests use diagrams to assess the ability to make logical decisions having studied a diagram (see Figure 1.11). They could involve deciphering a flowchart and deciding which step is not working properly. The tests are useful for maintenance or information technology de-bugging roles.

4 Spatial

Spatial tests assess the ability to mentally see a

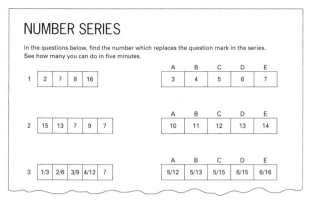

NUMBER SERIES

In the questions below, find the number which replaces the question mark in the series.
See how many you can do in five minutes.

						A	B	C	D	E
1	2	?	8	16		3	4	5	6	7

						A	B	C	D	E
2	15	13	?	9	7	10	11	12	13	14

						A	B	C	D	E
3	1/3	2/6	3/9	4/12	?	5/12	5/13	5/15	6/15	6/16

Figure 1.10: Example of numerical skills test, SHL Group PLC

two-dimensional drawing in three dimensions (see Figure 1.12). This skill is particularly important for designers. People who find Rubik's cube impossible or turn maps to face the way they are travelling probably lack this ability. There is some evidence that females overall have less ability in this area which may be one reason why there are less female engineers and designers.

5 Mechanical

Often used to recruit apprentices and engineering staff, the tests assess the ability to solve problems

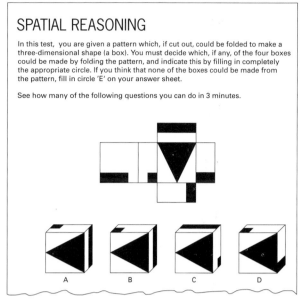

SPATIAL REASONING

In this test, you are given a pattern which, if cut out, could be folded to make a three-dimensional shape (a box). You must decide which, if any, of the four boxes could be made by folding the pattern, and indicate this by filling in completely the appropriate circle. If you think that none of the boxes could be made from the pattern, fill in circle 'E' on your answer sheet.

See how many of the following questions you can do in 3 minutes.

Figure 1.12: Example of spatial reasoning test, SHL Group PLC

involving mechanical principles (see Figure 1.13). Generally pictorial, mechanical tests are a good example of where both natural intelligence and some level of specific education is required. Clearly, these types of tests would not be suitable for many types of job, highlighting that matching the tests with the job is essential if they are to provide useful information.

6 Dexterity

These measure hand speed and fine precision skills.

Fault Finding

In this test you are required to follow sequences made up of a number of switches labelled A, B and C. Each of these switches, when working, has a specified effect on a set of numbered lights (shown in a square on the left). The circle on the right contains the result of a particular sequence. In each case, one of the switches is not working and so has no effect on the numbered lights. A list of the switches and what they do is shown below.

Switch	Effect when working
A	Turns 1 and 3 on/off i.e. from black to white or vice versa
B	Turns 3 and 4 on/off i.e. from black to white or vice versa
C	Turns 2 and 4 on/off i.e. from black to white or vice versa
	Remember — a switch that is not working has no effect

Your task is to identify the switch which is not working.

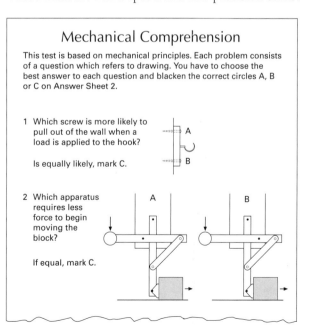

Figure 1.11: Example of diagrammatic reasoning test, SHL Group PLC

Mechanical Comprehension

This test is based on mechanical principles. Each problem consists of a question which refers to drawing. You have to choose the best answer to each question and blacken the correct circles A, B or C on Answer Sheet 2.

1 Which screw is more likely to pull out of the wall when a load is applied to the hook?

Is equally likely, mark C.

2 Which apparatus requires less force to begin moving the block?

If equal, mark C.

Figure 1.13: Example of mechanical comprehension test, SHL Group PLC

Primarily used for shopfloor employees, these tests are often designed by the employers rather than purchased from a testing company. The employer is able to utilize the types of components, tools and conditions under which they will actually be working.

For fine precision skills and dexterity with small objects, females are found to be more effective partly due to smaller fingers but it is also felt that they have better hand-to-eye co-ordination. Despite this fact, most surgeons are male!

7 Clerical

Jobs of all levels involve some clerical duties and tests cover areas such as checking for errors, filing or sorting computer files into directories

8 Sensory

Only used in jobs where visual or aural (sound) acuity is essential such as electrician, pilot or air traffic controller. One example is the Ishihara test of colour blindness given to all school children and at pre-employment medicals.

Test construction

Tests must be standardized if they are to be fair and give reliable and valid results. They must have the same:

- instructions
- timing
- scoring method
- interpretation
- questions.

The scores must be measured against a standardized norm group, that being a large sample of people who have taken the test prior to its use in the field.

Reliability

The reliability of a test is concerned with how precise it is as a measure. Any errors of measurement must be minimized (see Table 1.3).

Table 1.3: Examples of possible errors while testing

Factor	Example
Conditions	Room too hot
Administration instructions	Lack of standard instructions or straying from them
Scoring method	Using wrong marking method
Content	Poor or irrelevant questions
Temporary states	Candidate tired or ill

Reliability and validity

Reliability is particularly important as it affects the validity of a test. The validity is how relevant the test is to what is being measured. So it is possible to have a reliable measure (e.g. a ruler) but it would not be a valid way to assess the weight of something. A test can be reliable but not valid. A test cannot however be valid (e.g. scales for weighing), but not reliable (the scales are inaccurate).

Commentary

Reliability is getting the test right.
Validity is getting the right test.

The reliability of a test is expressed as a correlation called the reliability coefficient, and this figure is important when selecting a test. The reliability of a test can be assessed in various ways:

- **Test re test reliability** – the correlation between the scores that a group get on day one and when tested again on, for instance, day 30.
- **Alternate form reliability** – the correlation between the scores that a group get when they do one version of a test and then another.
- **Internal consistency reliability** – the consistency of all questions to test in a reliable manner. Comparing the results of the first half of the test with the second or odd and even questions can check this. If you calculate the coefficients for different ways of splitting the test and average them, you have calculated the **Cronbach Alpha**, a common reliability coefficient used in assessing tests.

Commentary

Bearing in mind that any reliability coefficients are an estimate, the tester should look to use tests with reliability coefficients of at least 0.7 by one or more of the above methods.

Validity

Any occupational assessment method is valid to the extent that it is relevant and predicts job and training performance. There are various types of validity:

- **Faith validity** – assuming that the test must be valid.
- **Content validity** – are the questions relevant to the content of the job?
- **Face validity** – on the 'face of it' the test looks valid.
- **Construct validity** – complex statistical tests

help the user decide if the test actually measures some theoretical construct such as spatial ability.

- **Empirical validity** – concerned with to what extent the test's performance correlates with job performance, possibly by comparing results with future appraisals or some measure of current performance. It is this form of validity that interests recruiters the most. One major study found that ability tests have a validity of 0.55. Ghiselli (1973) found a validity of +4.5 for training performance and +3.5 for job performance if the most appropriate test is selected. Examples of the validity of different selection methods are shown on p. 6.

Standard errors of measurement

While the reliability coefficient calculations cannot allow for the tester missing out instructions or other candidates causing distractions, they do allow for inevitable errors such as it is rarely possible for a question to be totally unambiguous. For instance, the question 'How old are you?' could be answered in years, days, approximately or in terms of how you feel.

These inevitable errors are dealt with by using a statistical tool called the **Standard Error of Measurement (SEM)**, which allows the tester to predict possible scores either side of that achieved or that the candidate could achieve if he or she was tested again.

Personality testing

In addition to intelligence or ability testing, personality is also assessed for many jobs. Probably even more controversial than using ability tests, assessing someone's personality, particularly if the recruiter is not trained, can be detrimental to the candidate and the reputation of the recruiting company. Personality testing is regarded by many as essential to the selection process, as simply to assess cognitive skills is too narrow and because personality should be a major predictor of job performance. Hogan (1990) summed up the importance of looking at personality when selecting an employee:

'There is an important difference between what a person can do and what he or she is willing to do.'

Validity studies between 1950 and 1970 showed poor validity for personality tests, yet since that time, successive studies have shown increased validity. The improvement is partly due to better test construction and training. In addition, personality questionnaires have focused historically on abnormal characteristics and were used for clinical assessment.

However, this type of questioning is of little use in assessing someone's likely performance in a job.

A further reason was that they tended to concentrate on inner dispositions rather than describing actual behaviour and, lastly, they were relatively easy to cheat on.

Beginnings of personality testing

Personality testing began in the field of clinical testing, with tests such as the Woodward Psychoneurotic Inventory, which was used to assess responses to stress, maladjustment and neurotic tendencies. It was designed to screen out soldiers who would be likely to suffer severe psychological disorders as a result of combat.

A more widely used clinical tool, the **Minnesota Multiphasic Personality Inventory** (MMPI), has also been used to select students for American universities and to aid the recruiting of police officers.

Personality tests increasingly became linked with 'the big five factors of personality' (Goldberg, 1993). These factors stem from many studies of the words used by people to describe others (see Figure 1.14): Allport and Odbert (1936) found 18 000; Warren Norman (1967) refined this to 2800; Thurstone (1938) found 1300.

The 'big five' influenced the construction of tests such as the 16PF and the OPQ, the difference being

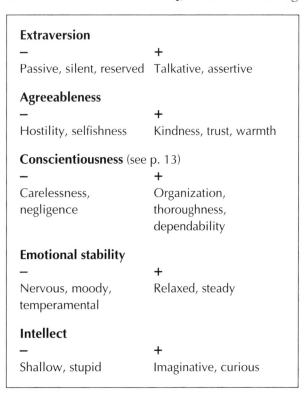

Extraversion	
–	**+**
Passive, silent, reserved	Talkative, assertive
Agreeableness	
–	**+**
Hostility, selfishness	Kindness, trust, warmth
Conscientiousness (see p. 13)	
–	**+**
Carelessness, negligence	Organization, thoroughness, dependability
Emotional stability	
–	**+**
Nervous, moody, temperamental	Relaxed, steady
Intellect	
–	**+**
Shallow, stupid	Imaginative, curious

Figure 1.14 The big five factors of personality

that these tests break down the 'big five' into different numbers of personality factors and don't necessarily use the same terminology as the 'big five'.

The 16PF, not surprisingly, has 16 factors and the OPQ has 30 grouped into three: thinking, feeling and relationships with people.

In the **OPQ32n** (the latest version of the OPQ) 230 statements are made and the user must indicate their agreement with each on a scale from 'strongly disagree' through to 'strongly agree'. The statements include:

- I like to take my time summing up situations.
- I do my own thing
- My feelings can easily be hurt.

Similar statements appear throughout the questionnaire to ascertain the strength and consistency of feeling. An example is shown in Figure 1.15. On either side are the descriptions of the behaviour being assessed and the preference for one or the other is shown by a mark on the scale. The shaded area on either side of the mark indicates the SEM.

The scores for each behaviour are given in **Stens** (a ranking scale). Stens 5 would be typical of most people in the norm group that the participant is being compared to.

Stens 5 or 6 – no particular preference for that behaviour.
Stens 4 and 7 – slight preference.
Stens 3 and 8 – definite preference.
Stens 2 and 9 – very strong preference.
Stens 1 and 10 – extreme preference.

The scores on different scales help build up an overall picture of the candidate as can be seen in Figure 1.15.

Derived from the personality theories of Carl Jung, the **Myers Briggs Indicator Test (MBIT)** is frequently used in occupational selection and interpersonal training. Once assessed, the candidate is given a four-letter profile linked with their scores on the scales shown in Figure 1.16). It is possible to purchase business cards, ties and desk tidies, with your name and your four-letter assessment. For example:

> *This is the desk of Michael Coates*
> *EFSJ*

Carl Jung

Most tests take 45 minutes and are increasingly being completed on computers rather than using traditional paper and pencil methods.

Bias and error

Psychometric tests are often criticized for their cultural and socio-economic bias, for instance:

> **Ability test**
> Knife is to fork as cup is to …

> **Personality questionnaire**
> I use a saucer with my cup of tea
> Always   Sometimes   Never

The middle-class writers of these questions may regularly drink tea from a cup and saucer, whereas many candidates will only get the cups out when Grandma visits! Questions therefore need to be culturally and class neutral.

Validity

The 16pf is a commonly used occupational assessment test but was originally designed for clinical uses and some would argue that this makes it less valid for occupational assessment.

Tests such as the Occupational Personality Ques-

Stens

#	Low	Scale	High	Category
RELATIONSHIPS WITH PEOPLE		1 2 3 4 5 6 7 8 9 10		
4	rarely pressures others to change their views, dislikes selling, less comfortable using negotiation	Persuasive	enjoys selling, comfortable using negotiation, likes to change other people's view	INFLUENCE
5	happy to let others take charge, dislikes telling people what to do, unlikely to take the lead	Controlling	likes to be in charge, takes the lead, tells others what to do, takes control	INFLUENCE
6	holds back from criticizing others, may not express own views, unprepared to put forward own opinions	Outspoken	freely expresses opinions, makes disagreement clear, prepared to criticize others	INFLUENCE
4	accepts majority decisions, prepared to follow the consensus	Independent Minded	prefers to follow own approach, prepared to disregard majority decisions	INFLUENCE
4	quiet and reserved in groups, dislikes being centre of attention	Outgoing	lively and animated in groups, talkative, enjoys attention	SOCIABILITY
4	comfortable spending time away from people, values time spent alone, seldom misses the company of others	Affiliative	enjoys others' company, likes to be around people, can miss the company of others	SOCIABILITY
7	feels more comfortable in less formal situations, can feel awkward when first meeting people	Socially Confident	feels comfortable when first meeting people, at ease in formal situations	SOCIABILITY
5	makes strengths and achievements known, talks about personal success	Modest	dislikes discussing achievements, keeps quiet about personal success	EMPATHY
9	prepared to make decisions without consultation, prefers to make decisions alone	Democratic	consults widely, involves others in decision making, less likely to make decisions alone	EMPATHY
1	selective with sympathy and support, remains detached from others' personal problems	Caring	sympathetic and considerate towards others, helpful and supportive, gets involved in others' problems	EMPATHY
THINKING STYLE		1 2 3 4 5 6 7 8 9 10		
10	prefers dealing with opinions and feelings rather than facts and figures, likely to avoid using statistics	Data Rational	likes working with numbers, enjoys analysing statistical information, bases decisions on facts and figures	ANALYSIS
10	does not focus on potential limitations, dislikes critically analysing information, rarely looks for errors or mistakes	Evaluative	critically evaluates information, looks for potential limitations, focuses upon errors	ANALYSIS
3	does not question the reasons for people's behaviour, tends not to analyse people	Behavioural	tries to understand motives and behaviours, enjoys analysing people	ANALYSIS
4	favours changes to work methods, prefers new approaches, less conventional	Conventional	prefers well-established methods, favours a more conventional approach	CREATIVITY AND CHANGE
9	prefers to deal with practical rather than theoretical issues, dislikes dealing with abstract concepts	Conceptual	interested in theories, enjoys discussing abstract concepts	CREATIVITY AND CHANGE
5	more likely to build on than generate ideas, less inclined to be creative and inventive	Innovative	generates new ideas, enjoys being creative, thinks of original solutions	CREATIVITY AND CHANGE
5	prefers routine, is prepared to do repetitive work, does not seek variety	Variety Seeking	prefers variety, tries out new things, likes changes to regular routine, can become bored by repetitive work	CREATIVITY AND CHANGE
3	behaves consistently across situations, unlikely to behave differently with different people	Adaptable	changes behaviour to suit the situation, adapts approach to different people	CREATIVITY AND CHANGE
5	more likely to focus upon immediate than long-term issues, less likely to take a strategic perspective	Forward Thinking	takes a long-term view, sets goals for the future, more likely to take a strategic perspective	STRUCTURE
7	unlikely to become preoccupied with detail, less organized and systematic, dislikes tasks involving detail	Detail Conscious	focuses on detail, likes to be methodical, organized and systematic, may become preoccupied with detail	STRUCTURE
5	sees deadlines as flexible, prepared to leave some tasks unfinished	Conscientious	focuses on getting things finished, persists until the job is done	STRUCTURE
6	not restricted by rules and procedures, prepared to break rules, tends to dislike bureaucracy	Rule Following	follows rules and regulations, prefers clear guidelines, finds it difficult to break rules	STRUCTURE
FEELINGS AND EMOTIONS		1 2 3 4 5 6 7 8 9 10		
7	tends to feel tense, finds it difficult to relax, can find it hard to unwind after work	Relaxed	finds it easy to relax, rarely feels tense, generally calm and untroubled	EMOTION
4	feels calm before important occasions, less affected by key events, free from worry	Worrying	feels nervous before important occasions, worries about things going wrong	EMOTION
7	sensitive, easily hurt by criticism, upset by unfair comments or insults	Tough Minded	not easily offended, can ignore insults, may be insensitive to personal criticism	EMOTION
3	concerned about the future, expects things to go wrong, focuses on negative aspects of a situation	Optimistic	expects things will turn out well, looks to the positive aspects of a situation, has an optimistic view of the future	EMOTION
5	wary of others' intentions, finds it difficult to trust others, unlikely to be fooled by people	Trusting	trusts people, sees others as reliable and honest, believes what others say	EMOTION
6	openly expresses feelings, finds it difficult to conceal feelings, displays emotion clearly	Emotionally Controlled	can conceal feelings from others, rarely displays emotion	EMOTION
6	likes to take things at a steady pace, dislikes excessive work demands	Vigorous	thrives on activity, likes to keep busy, enjoys having a lot to do	DYNAMISM
7	dislikes competing with others, feels that taking part is more important than winning	Competitive	has a need to win, enjoys competitive activities, dislikes losing	DYNAMISM
7	sees career progression as less important, looks for achievable rather than highly ambitious targets	Achieving	ambitious and career-centred, likes to work to demanding goals and targets	DYNAMISM
3	tends to be cautious when making decisions, likes to take time to reach conclusions	Decisive	makes fast decisions, reaches conclusions quickly, less cautious	DYNAMISM
4	has responded less consistently across the questionnaire	Consistency	has responded more consistently across the questionnaire	

OPQ32I Undergrads 1999

1 2 3 4 5 6 7 8 9 10

Figure 1.15: Example of combinations of OPQ scales, SHL Group PLC

Introversion Reserved, withdrawn, passive	*Extraversion* Sociable, friendly, talkative
Thinking Rational, likes order A sunset is a sunset	*Feeling* Emphasis on emotion A sunset produces an emotional response
Intuition Where it comes from and where it is going Concerned with future possibilities	*Sensing* Perception, knowing something exists
Judging Prefers control and making decisions	*Perceiving* Open to experiences

Figure 1.16: The scales used in MBIT

tionnaire (OPQ) are, as the name suggests, designed to assess someone's personality in a work setting, reflecting that people may act differently at work. Tests continue to be revised to reflect better the occupational side of personality and this is one factor in their steadily improving validity ratings. For instance, in 1999 the OPQ had a personality dimension called 'Active', i.e. has energy, moves quickly, enjoys physical exercise. In the latest version, OPQ32, this has been removed, as it was unclear what relevance this had to the workplace.

Cheating

It is commonly believed that it is possible to cheat on personality questionnaires, particularly if the candidate has done a few or is trained to interpret them. This is countered in various ways.

Numerous questions are inserted to act as 'lie detectors', e.g. 'I never gossip about others': True, Somewhat true, Not true of me, etc. Test subjects with nothing to gain from lying are given these questions and subsequent candidates have their responses compared to these norm tables.

Personality questionnaires should always be followed up with a discussion between the subject and a trained tester. This discussion may elicit reasons why the candidate answered as he or she did and add a different slant to its interpretation.

Ipsitive models, where the user ranks totally unrelated statements, are also available and they are harder to manipulate but also more tedious to complete.

What is looked for?

While there is no ideal personality, there are personality characteristics that may be felt to be more beneficial or essential for particular roles. These would be identified during a job analysis and would appear on the position profile. For instance, with a salesperson, the test would be looking for high scores for 'Outgoing, socially confident, innovative, etc.'

Emotional intelligence (EI)

Emotional intelligence (EI) is increasingly being regarded along with intelligence and personality as an aspect to examine at the selection stage. Due to the popularity of this new 'theory' and the money being injected into the training and products that have been spawned by it, there is some debate over who first identified it. Dr John Mayer of the University of New Hampshire wrote articles on emotional intelligence in 1990, but it was the publication of the book *Emotional intelligence* by Dr Daniel Goleman (1995) that brought it to the public's attention. Mayer described EI as now being:

'a product of two worlds. One is the popular culture world of best selling books, newspapers and magazines. The other is the world of scientific journals, book chapters and peer review'.

Time magazine said that EI 'may be the best predictor of success in life' and Goleman's book (1995) states that:

'evidence suggests that it is powerful and at times more powerful than IQ and provides an advantage to any domain of life'.

So what is this seemingly amazing predictor of success? Daniel Goleman studied the competency models used by 188 large organizations including British Airways and Credit Suisse. His studies identified that of the competencies required for most managerial roles, the 'soft' or people-related skills were twice as important as IQ or technical skills. The importance of these skills rose dramatically as he looked at higher levels of organization whereas previously it had always been the correlation between IQ and status that had been publicized.

Goleman grouped these competencies into five broad areas (see Table 1.4)

Goleman and others maintain that displaying these competencies will bring about greater success, not just at work but in relationships and even bringing up children. With this in mind, employers were

Table 1.4: The five components of emotional intelligence at work

Component	Definition	Hallmarks
Self-awareness	The ability to recognize and understand your moods, emotions, and drives, as well as their effect on others	Self-confidence Realistic self-assessment Self-deprecating sense of humour
Self-regulation	The ability to control or redirect disruptive impulses and moods The propensity to suspend judgment – to think before acting	Trustworthiness and integrity Comfort with ambiguity Openness to change
Motivation	A passion to work for the reasons that go beyond money or status A propensity to pursue goals with energy and persistence	Strong drive to achieve Optimism, even in the face of failure Organizational commitment
Empathy	The ability to understand the emotional makeup of other people Skill in treating people according to their emotional reactions	Expertise in building and retaining talent Cross-cultural sensitivity Service to clients and customers
Social skill	Proficiency in managing relationships and building networks An ability to find common ground and build rapport	Effectiveness in leading change Persuasiveness Expertise in building and leading teams

faced with two dilemmas. How do they identify who has these skills? Can they be developed?

Goleman (and now most of the major personality questionnaire companies) have developed tests to assess an individual's EI and give a figure for it, called the Emotional Quotient or EQ. So while it is now relatively easy to test for EI, can it be learned? Goleman maintains that it can. While he acknowledges that many people are born with greater EI than others (nature), he is convinced that our environment allows us to develop these skills (nurture). In particular, EI develops naturally with age but people can be trained in it. Goleman believes that many training courses miss the point as they develop the wrong part of the brain:

'EI is born largely in the neurotransmitters of the brain's limbic system, which governs feelings, impulses and drives. Research indicates that the limbic system learns best through motivation, extended practice and feedback. As opposed to the neo cortex which governs analytical and technical ability' (Goleman, 1995).

He believes that by having training courses that involve analysis and theories, the wrong part of the brain is used.

Instead training should emphasize people getting to understand their shortcomings and encourage feedback from others even if it is not pleasant. Then they should be coached and practise their new skills with regular feedback, only then will they develop the EI skills.

Commentary

Unfortunately, such training is very time consuming and expensive. Without the full co-operation of the 'trainee' it will also be ineffective, which admittedly is also true of traditional training, but at least then the majority of the class was probably learning. What EI has done though is change the emphasis of what is being looked for as a determinate of success, from the technical side of a job to the people skills aspect (see RLA 2).

Real Life Application 2: American Express uses EI

Long before Daniel Goleman published his best seller, American Express Financial Advisors (AEFA) had been tapping into the power of emotional intelligence.

In 1992, AEFA researched why only 28 per cent of customers the company advised had purchased life insurance. The results showed that there appeared to be a direct correlation between the emotional intelligence of the financial advisor and business success. It was hypothesized that if financial decisions are driven by emotions such as pride, trust and a sense of security rather than facts and figures, then developing the emotional intelligence of financial advisors should increase business.

After a training programme designed to help

managers develop a greater awareness of customer's and their own emotional reactions, those who participated grew their business by 18.1 per cent as opposed to 16.2 per cent by non participants. Eighty-eight per cent of those who completed the training believe that EI is important to business performance. As of 1996 all new advisors at AEFA have been trained in EI.

Article adapted from 'American Express taps into the power of emotional intelligence' by Scott Hays, *Workforce magazine* (USA), July 1999.

Summary

- AEFA identified the motives behind financial purchases as being emotional rather than rational.
- By responding and communicating in those terms, financial advisors appear to have been more successful.

Questions

1 What other factors may have been responsible for the increase in business by participants?

2 What other job roles do you think might benefit from this approach?

Spiritual intelligence

In the spring of 2000, newspaper articles started to appear referring to the 'God Spot' having been found and that people have 'spiritual intelligence'. This came about from research that found there is a part of the frontal lobe of the brain that when artificially excited, causes the test subject to have deep spiritual experiences and often to have religious visions. It was therefore concluded that this part of the brain controls a person's spirituality, thereby explaining why some have a far deeper-rooted faith than others. The phrase 'Spiritual Quotient' or SQ (Zohar, 2000) then appeared alongside IQ and the relatively new EQ.

SQ, it is said, concerns a person's passion or commitment:

'evidenced by a traditional religious belief, but also by your own private desires, your love of your family and friends and your commitment to whatever belief system you have. You can be spiritually wealthy and be an atheist' (Zohar, 2000).

Zohar maintains that if a person has a high SQ they will be far more productive, yet despite this, managers tend not to encourage people to act passionately or to think independently.

Commentary

Critics would say that despite the neurophysiological evidence, SQ is leaping on the bandwagon of EQ and is another fad for which companies will pay a fortune to learn more. Others would say that the elements of personality described, are often in existing competency models.

As yet, SQ is not assessed at selection interviews.

Other methods of selection

Interviewing

By far the most common method of selection (80 per cent of all selection), interviewing is also commonly misused. Interviews can be very stressful for both parties. However, there is evidence that a well carried out interview actually reduces this stress. A traditional interview has a very low validity, begging the question 'Why bother?'. It need not be that way if interviewers are trained to use the following technique.

- Ensure that a thorough job analysis, person specification and CV screening has taken place. The shortlist of candidates should on paper at least all seem good matches with the ideal profile.
- Use psychometric tests prior to interviewing to screen out more candidates. If tests are done after the first interview they should influence who gets a second.
- Prepare in advance a set of questions such as the following:
  - Briefly, please talk me through your CV, highlighting achievements relevant to this job.
  - Why did you join your current company?
  - With examples, please describe your effectiveness in your current job.
  - If your company has an appraisal system, please describe the major successes it covers.
  - What development needs were identified at your appraisal?
- Add to this list questions relating to some of the competencies required. The questions should be worded so that the candidate must give examples of when they have displayed that competence rather than questions about how they might do so. The following is one example:

> **Competency**
> *Gathering and utilizing information*
> 1 Describe how you organize your day.
> 2 Using actual examples describe how you establish priorities.
> 3 Briefly explain the most complex analytical challenge you have faced and say how you tackled it.
> 4 Provide a recent example of where you have had to evaluate a system or procedure.

Figure 1.17: Negative body language

- Analyse each CV and highlight areas of interest. Be familiar with the CVs, thereby avoiding asking inane questions such as 'Have you ever done any selling?' when the CV states 'Salesperson of the Year, 1995–2000'.
- Choose the venue carefully. It should be quiet, not too hot or cold, with phones switched off. Arrange the room so that any barriers such as a desk are not directly between the interviewer and candidate. Barriers create an oppressive atmosphere and hide body language.
- Make sure the candidate has clear directions and timings.
- Start the interview with some small talk to let the candidate settle in.
- The interviewer should explain who he or she is, provide some information about the company and then describe the job.
- Do not use closed questions unless as a lead in to an open one. For example, 'Are you good at communicating?' is likely to receive a heartfelt 'yes', whereas a question such as 'Give me an example of where your communication skills have helped a situation' is more likely to provide evidence that the candidate does use this skill. This is called **situational** or **behavioural interviewing** and became more widely used in the light of work by Latham and Saari (1984). Behavioural interviews have a validity of 0.32 (see p. 6).
- Probe answers with questions such as:
  - Why did you do it that way?
  - What effect did this have?
  - What feedback did you receive?
  - What would you do differently next time?
  Probing helps the interviewer to gather more evidence that the example was real and that the candidate has reflected on his or her experiences in order to learn.

- Once the candidate has answered, use silence to make him or her continue. Often this continuation will contain a level of honesty the individual would ordinarily not have given.
- Watch the candidate's **body language** or **non-verbal cues**. While body language should never be interpreted in isolation, if it contradicts the words that are being spoken, then follow up questions should be used. Alan Pease (1981) maintains that 70 per cent of the actual message we receive from others is via non-verbal cues. To ignore these in an interview situation is to allow vital pieces of evidence to pass by.

Examples of body language in an interview (Pease, 1981)

If the candidate creates a barrier by crossing his or her legs and arms (see Figure 1.17), the interviewer should mirror this position (copy the candidate's actions), then drop eye contact, sit forward, adjust the legs and arms to an open position, to which the candidate is likely to mirror this more open position.

If the candidate touches his or her face, ears or mouth while answering a question, this may indicate that he or she is uncomfortable with the answer he or she is giving (see Figure 1.18). The touching of the face is thought to be due to skin sensations caused by a rise in blood pressure. The touching of the mouth when lying is thought to be a version of the child-like

Figure 1.18: Possible indications that candidates are uncomfortable with the answers they are giving

Figure 1.19: Body language of an over-confident candidate

behaviour to cover the mouth while lying. Probing questions should definitely be used if a question causes the candidate to touch his or her face, drop eye contact and cross his or her legs or arms.

On the other hand, some candidates may be a little too confident (see Figure 1.19).

Remember though, body language is only a guide to understanding responses; it can easily be misinterpreted.

Bias in interviews

Bias must also be avoided. It is very easy to be biased when actually meeting the candidate, due to an interpretation of his or her appearance, particularly if the individual makes a striking first impression. There is evidence that many people (quite wrongly) make quick character stereotypical assumptions in light of appearance, for instance:

- fat = lazy
- blonde and female = less intelligent
- male and tattoos = violent and less intelligent
- casually dressed = not professional
- not attractive = whole range of negative feelings.

Esses and Webster (1988) found that test subjects consistently painted less-attractive sex offenders as more dangerous than others, when shown photographs. Nisbett and Wilson (1977) found that students provided far more positive responses to films of lecturers who acted in a 'warm' manner than a 'cold' one. Even though the content of the lectures was the same, the students consistently felt that the content of the lecture and the skills of the lecturer were better. Studies of children in schools show that they also respond better to attractive teachers.

Interviewers need to take great care that they are actually judging the candidate on the evidence before them and not due to any stereotyping or subconscious impression caused by appearance, manner or accent. The 'halo or horns' bias is an example of this and can first appear at the CV screening stage when candidates who have one strong feature are shortlisted even though weaknesses are apparent elsewhere (halo). Alternatively, a CV that is not in the preferred format may mean that the recruiter 'looks down' on the candidate's application (horns). At interview, candidates who share common interests, education or background with the interviewer may be treated more favourably, while those with nothing in common may find it difficult to impress.

Another form of error is the recency effect, where the positive answers at the end of the interview are

Table 1.5: Example of assessment centre evidence analysis

	In-tray exercise	Group exercise	Presentation	Aptitude tests
Analysis	Primary			Secondary
Communication		Secondary	Primary	
Supporting others	Secondary	Primary		
Prioritizing	Primary	Secondary		

remembered, whereas the negative ones at the start are not (or visa versa) or remembering the final candidate but not remembering the first.

Commentary

Philips and Dipboyne (1989) and Robbins (1991) made further criticisms of interviewing:

- Interviewers make inaccurate perceptual judgements.
- Different interviewers come to different conclusions.
- Interviewers make quick first impressions.
- Prior knowledge of the candidate clouds their judgement.
- The halo effect exists particularly if the candidate shares similar interests, upbringing or education as the interviewer.
- Negative information is given greater weighting than positive.
- That an applicant's ability to do well in an interview is not a reflection of how well he or she will do in the job.

Graham and Bennet (1974) also warn interviewers against asking:

- leading questions, e.g. 'I suppose that was a great success?'
- questions that contain multiple questions
- questions that are lengthy and confusing
- rude or insensitive questions

Alternative methods of selection

Assessment centres

Used extensively for graduate recruitment, assessment centres utilize multiple assessment methods and have the highest validity of any selection technique. Candidates are assessed by multiple assessors, can interact with each other and are assessed against pre-set criteria. Each exercise will be identified as providing primary evidence and possible secondary evidence and there will be at least one primary provider for each competency being looked for (see Table 1.5).

Assessors are looking for actual evidence of that competency being displayed using a process known as **ORCE**:

Observe Watch.
Record Write down what the candidate does.
Classify Allocate the observations, if possible, to one of the competencies being observed.
Evaluate Decide whether the observations provide good, average or weak evidence of that competence.

Candidates will be observed by different assessors for each exercise, thereby reducing bias. Having multiple assessors does, however, make assessment centres a very costly and time-consuming activity.

Biodata

Controversial due to lack of validity, biodata involves allocating points depending upon certain responses, either on the application form or from a questionnaire. For example, for an accountant, four years in a similar role will score highly, whereas three years as a chef will not. Studies such as Asher (1972) have demonstrated that biodata is a useful method if used properly, however often the links between the answers given and points awarded is tentative, e.g. 'plays in the pub Rugby team' does not necessarily deserve high points for 'teamwork'.

In reality this method is used instinctively when screening candidates at CV stage.

Graphology

Graphology is the study of handwriting and is often used in France as a method of selection. Despite there being no evidence of its validity, the author has had his handwriting analysed and found the result to be frighteningly accurate!

Large loops under the line are supposed to mean

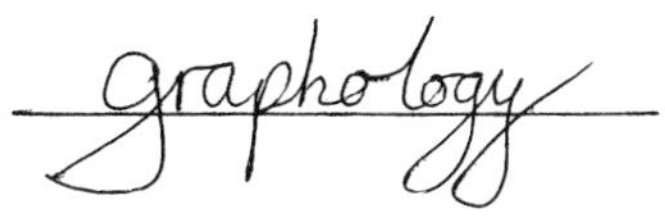

Figure 1.20: Writing such as this would lead a graphologist to conclude that the candidate is outgoing

that the person is very outgoing and confident both socially and sexually! (see Figure 1.20)

The British Psychological Society in 1994 concluded:

'There is no evidence to support the claims of graphology and there is no relationship at all between what graphology predicts and subsequent performance in the work place.'

Astrology

There is some evidence that astrological profiles are produced to aid selection. However, validity is no higher than probability would predict.

Poligraphy

Lie detectors are commonly used in criminal cases and have been used to assess the integrity of job candidates. They are not, however, infallible (Hall and Goodale, 1986). Legislation in many countries now bans their use in job selection. Instead, written integrity questionnaires are used. They contain questions such as 'I have never stolen anything from work'. There is evidence that those who do steal will answer that they have because they assume everyone does. Hogan (1990) examined the most commonly used tests and found them to be either broad or narrow in focus. Broad focus tests view theft and dishonesty as specific examples of counterproductive

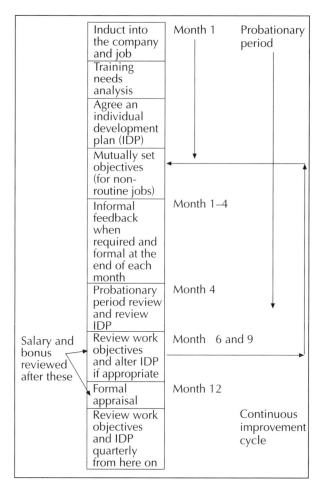

Induct into the company and job	Month 1	Probationary period
Training needs analysis		
Agree an individual development plan (IDP)		
Mutually set objectives (for non-routine jobs)		
Informal feedback when required and formal at the end of each month	Month 1–4	
Probationary period review and review IDP	Month 4	
Review work objectives and alter IDP if appropriate	Month 6 and 9	
Formal appraisal	Month 12	
Review work objectives and IDP quarterly from here on		Continuous improvement cycle

Salary and bonus reviewed after these

Figure 1.21: Typical appraisal process
IDP = Individual development (training) plan

behaviour that might include drug abuse or sabotage, however the questions disguise the behaviour they are aiming at identifying. Narrow focus surveys ask specific questions about attitudes towards dishonest behaviours, i.e. questions are overtly about that behaviour.

Only broadly focused tests have been found to have any useful validity (Goldberg *et al*,1991) and Hogan (1989).

Appraisal systems

Once an employee has been selected for employment, the process shown in Figure 1.21 should be followed to help ensure the individual's effectiveness and retention.

Commentary

The importance of providing regular and constructive feedback cannot be over stressed, particularly for new employees. It is a skill that many managers lack or simply do not have the time to carry out and as a result employees are often surprised at their appraisal or when

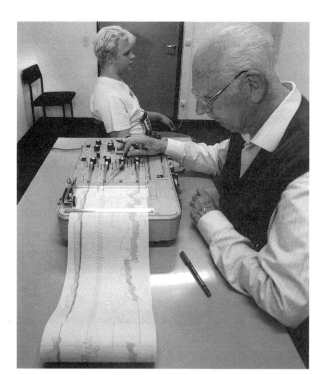

A polygraph test

Outcome feedback
- B+ at the bottom of an essay.
- Exam results.
- 'Congratulations, Miss Hooda, you have passed your driving test.'
- 'I am sorry to inform you that you have not passed your driving test.'
- 'Well done on getting the new account, we are all delighted.'
- 'I am sorry but I do not want to go out with you any more.'

Process feedback
- B+ at the bottom of the essay plus 'You explained the theories of feedback well and the use of examples made it much clearer for the reader'.
- 'Congratulations, Miss Hooda, you have passed your driving test. I was particularly impressed by the way you turned the car using forward and reverse gears in such a narrow road.'
- 'Well done on getting the new account. I hear that you were the only salesperson to spend time with the end users of the equipment, so you really understood their needs. That really made the difference.'
- 'I am sorry but I don't want to go out with you any more. Your body odour problem does nothing for me.'

Figure 1.22: Examples of outcome and process feedback

disciplined, because it is the first time they have heard that their performance is not satisfactory.

Giving feedback

McAffee *et al* (1995) identified two forms of feedback: **outcome feedback**, i.e. information regarding whether a standard was met or not, and **process feedback**, i.e. information concerning the effectiveness of the work method used (see Figure 1.22). They contend that process feedback is the most constructive in encouraging continuous improvement and go on to test the hypothesis that employees receiving both types of feedback will not only experience improved performance but job satisfaction too. Their results indicate that providing discretion alone (a person's ability to have some control over his or her work methods and targets) does not improve job satisfaction significantly, however providing discretion with both types of feedback results in significant improvements.

Erez (1977) also found that providing feedback had an impact on performance.

Appraisals

Normally held once or twice a year, appraisals are a formal opportunity for a manager to feed back to individual employees and to hear how they feel that they have done and where they see themselves going. They often help to clear up misunderstandings and re-establish the **psychological contract** (see p. 53). Appraisals can also help the manager to decide on levels of performance-related salary or bonus and whether that employee should be promoted or demoted. Development needs are often identified and if done properly in an integrated system, they would be used to validate the initial selection process (see Figure 1.2).

In real life, appraisals are often a rushed (or omitted) meeting, in which the manager simply provides bland non-specific feedback. Such appraisals lead to the employee seeing the process as a waste of time. Poor appraisals are very demotivating to individual employees if:

- they feel they performed better than the manager believes (Heneman, 1974)
- there was little opportunity to counter any criticisms
- factors out of their control went against them
- the manager was ill prepared
- as a result of an unfair appraisal, salary/bonus or promotion was adversely affected
- the appraiser is not credible.

Appraisals are not essential in themselves if regular feedback and development planning is carried out. However, if an appraisal system does exist, it must be handled well, otherwise it can be very counterproductive.

Performance appraisal methods
Individual evaluation (unrelated to the performance of others)

This is often just a few paragraphs about the person's achievements, a bit like a school report.

Rating scales

Customer skills
Excellent
✓ Good
Fair
Poor

Rating scales in appraisals are very common and often lead to disagreements between the two parties and significant differences between different appraisers' ratings can be seen. If salary levels are dependent upon certain grades, 'hard or lenient' markers could affect the salaries significantly. Despite these criticisms, rating scales have been around for some time and are still very popular particularly for shopfloor appraisals.

Behaviourally anchored rating scales (BARS)

These are similar to rating scales, but each rating has a description attached clearly explaining the types of behaviour or output that would need to have been seen consistently throughout the year in order to achieve that rating (see Figure 1.23).

Competency-communication

1　Communicates necessary information when required. Listens when important information is being discussed. Both written and verbal communications contain relevant information.

2　Both written and verbal communications are clear and in language that aids understanding. Listens attentively and asks questions to clarify points. Relays information accurately.

3　Tailors the style, content and pace of communication to suit the situation or person. Identifies information that others may require and ensures that they receive it. Questions information to ensure that it is relevant, accurate and interpreted correctly. Provides regular updates to those who require it.

4　Is a very effective communicator, always using the correct media, thereby providing accurate, concise, timely and clear information to others. Communicates easily and effectively with all audiences and inspires a feeling of trust in those that they communicate to, particularly on the accuracy of information.

Figure 1.23: Example of BARS

Commentary

BAR scales are a far less subjective method of rating an individual's performance. There may still be some dispute over ratings and managers can still ignore the evidence in front of them but overall they offer a more effective solution if written correctly.

BAR scales must show tangible differences between each rating if ambiguity is to be avoided. They are more expensive to develop due to their complexity and they may need regular updating as jobs change, particularly with the progressive application of information and communications technology in people roles. Also, managers face difficulty if they cannot find a rating that matches the individual

Comparative evaluation

If all employees more than meet their targets, then salary and bonus payments would be very high if linked to these rankings. This might be affordable if the targets were linked with company profits but many employees in support roles, e.g. administration, catering, etc. are a cost, not a profit centre in the business.

If all employees receive high rankings it could be that:

- the company has an excellent selection and development process (this is rare)
- the targets were set too low
- the appraisals were too generous.

A comparative ranking system compares the results, skills and weaknesses within a group and using evidence of performance, all the employees are rated as a 1, 2, 3, 4 (1 being high performers, 4 being a very poor performer compared to the others).

Forced ranking

From an analysis of BARS scores it is possible to draw up a distribution curve showing the number of employees who scored each of the ratings. Typically, if you have a large enough group, performance will produce a normal distribution curve, (sometimes called a **bell curve** – see Figure 1.24) with most people scoring a 3 (as good as most people) and less getting 5 (better than most) or 1 (worse than most).

In forced ranking only a certain percentage of employees *can* be awarded the highest rating and a

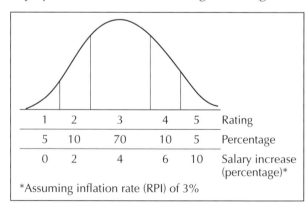

Rating	1	2	3	4	5
Percentage	5	10	70	10	5
Salary increase (percentage)*	0	2	4	6	10

*Assuming inflation rate (RPI) of 3%

Figure 1.24: Normal distribution/bell curve showing how forced ranking can link with salary increases

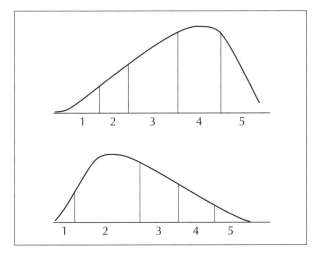

Figure 1.25: What might cause distribution curves like these?

certain percentage *must* receive the lowest rating. The principle being that in any group if you compare performance to each other, there will be a few who excel and a few who may be doing a good job but compared to everyone else are lagging. Salary or bonuses reflect the rankings.

Forced ranking can only be done for large groups, preferably over 25. In a small team of excellent performers, one would still have to be rated as very poor.

Commentary

The purpose of forced ranking is to ensure that top per-

formers see a greater improvement in their salary than average or poor performers. The process is criticized, as managers are often forced to downgrade people in order to fit them into the distribution curve, even though the evidence supports them having a higher ranking. In order to make the groups large enough, the appraisals of numerous departments may need to be looked at together and they would have been ranked by different appraisers with different viewpoints

Multi rator

Commonly called 360° appraisal as it involves anonymous feedback from:

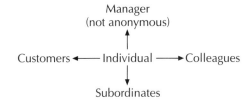

These can be simple questionnaires but often they are commercially produced and based around either a generic competency model or the company's own model. Figure 1.26 is an example of a competency model with its competency definition and some typical questions. In this Profilor model by Personnel Decisions International there are over 200 questions that can be completed either on paper questionnaires or online. Once all of the feedback is collated, an extensive report is produced and trained facilitators

Forced ranking can lead to inappropriate ranking

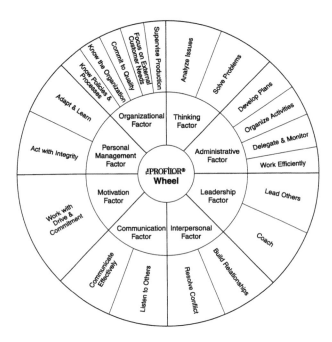

THINKING FACTOR

1. Analyze Issues: Looks beyond symptoms to identify causes of problems; analyzes problems from different points of view; does not get bogged down in detail; draws accurate conclusions from quantitative information.
2. Solve Problems: Considers possible causes of problems; generates alternative or innovative solutions; makes sound decisions; acts quickly and decisively when needed; uses a team approach to solve problems when appropriate.

ADMINISTRATIVE FACTOR

3. Develop Plans: Develops plans that are realistic, thorough, and effective in meeting goals; integrates planing efforts with other units and broader initiatives.
4. Organize Activities: Mobilizes people by directing their activities; sets priorities for others; ensures that work is completed on schedule.
5. Delegate and Monitor: Clearly assigns responsibilities and tasks to others; establishes effective controls and monitors progress; ensures that employees have necessary resources and authority.
6. Work Efficiently: Approaches work in a methodical manner; addresses problems according to priority; plans own work and schedules activities so that deadlines and objectives are met.

LEADERSHIP FACTOR

7. Lead Others: Takes charge and initiates actions; directs the activities of individuals and groups toward accomplishment of meaningful goals; pulls work group together into a coherent team; commands attention and respect of others.
8. Coach: Evaluates employees; provides performance feedback; facilitates professional growth.

INTERPERSONAL FACTOR

9. Build Relationships: Views people positively; builds strong working relationships with people at all levels in the organization; accepts individual differences and shortcomings nonjudgmentally.

10. Resolve Conflict: Brings conflict into the open and attempts to resolve while maintaining positive working relationships; finds ways to compromise; builds consensus when needed.

COMMUNICATION FACTOR

11. Listen to Others: Listens closely to others; demonstrates an interest in and understanding of what others are saying.
12. Communicate Effectively: Keeps people informed of decisions, changes, and other relevant information on a timely basis; writes clearly.

MOTIVATION FACTOR

13. Work with Drive and Commitment: Sets high standards of personal performance; sets challenging goals and works hard to achieve them; shows commitment to organizational change efforts.

PERSONAL MANAGEMENT FACTOR

14. Act with Integrity: Acts ethically and honestly; behaves according to stated values; builds trust with others by demonstrating consistency between words and actions.
15. Adapt and Learn: Remains effective in high pressure circumstances; maintains composure; learns from feedback and experience.

ORGANIZATION FACTOR

16. Know Policies and Processes: Knows and applies essential policies and processes.
17. Know the Organization: Shows understanding of other parts of the organization and external issues that are relevant to the business.
18. Commit to Quality: Delivers quality products and/or services; enforces adherence to quality standards; achieves balance between need to meet both productivity goals and quality standards.
19. Supervise Production: Oversees the production process to ensure that capacity demands and quality standards are met.
20. Focus on External Customer Needs: Takes appropriate action to meet external customer needs; looks for ways to increase customer satisfaction and takes action accordingly.

Figure 1.26: Profilor competency wheel and definitions

feed back this information in order to help the individual alter his or her development plan.

360° appraisals are particularly effective for development planning but less so for performance appraisals, as individuals may not want to provide low ratings if they know it will affect someone's salary. Alternatively, if they know that only 10 per cent of employees can get a decent salary rise they may be tempted to downgrade their colleague in order to give themselves a better chance. There is also some evidence that friends give more favourable ratings (DeNisi and Mitchell, 1978) and that popular people tend to get more favourable ratings.

They do have the advantage though that they get multiple inputs rather than only the manager's and they revolve around specific competencies rather than just vague statements about how someone has done. They can be expensive though and very time consuming as up to ten people need to complete them just to produce one report on an individual.

Bias, reliability and validity

Whatever the form of appraisal, the same reliability and validity factors described on p. 16 for selection techniques apply. In addition, there are similar opportunities for bias such as the halo effect where popular employees or ones who have achieved recent successes find that weaknesses are down played in their appraisals. In addition, the mood of the appraiser at the time of writing it can have an influence.

Grading errors occur due to the personality of appraisers. If they get on well with the individual or if they know the person will cause trouble if he or she receives a poor appraisal, they may be more lenient.

The timing of the appraisal is also important. It may be biased if it comes straight after a major success or failure or if the appraisal reflects events that were a long time ago or if the appraisal only reflects recent events (recency effect).

Worst of all is the often subconscious but sometimes deliberate bias against people of other cultures, generations or sex. The 'glass ceiling' is a phrase often used to describe how groups, particularly females, can see the promotions but can't get there, often due to the influence that male managers have over their appraisals. Multi-rater appraisals reduce these opportunities for bias.

Essay questions

1a Ability or aptitude tests are often used during employee selection. What factors should be considered when selecting such tests? (10)

1b 'Aptitude testing is controversial when used to select employees'. Discuss. (13)

2a Many personality questionnaires are based on 'the big five'. What are the big five? (10)

2b The validity of personality questionnaires has improved in recent years. Discuss how this has been achieved. (13)

3 'Emotional intelligence is by far the most important factor to consider when selecting an employee.' Discuss. (23)

2 Feelings at work

This chapter discusses why people are motivated to go to work in the first place and what motivates them once they get there. One of those factors is, of course, money and different reward mechanisms are described. Then it covers some of the demotivating elements of work, such as stress and redundancy. Real Life Applications that are considered are:

- RLA3: NHS faces worst staffing crisis in 26 years
- RLA4: Britons are most dissatisfied workers in Europe
- RLA5: Work and family.

Why do we work?

Work allows us not only to ensure our physical survival but it helps to transform the environment in which we live, our home, our social circles, the places we visit. Watson (1980) states that:

'work is basic to the ways in which human beings deal with the scarcity of resources available in the environment and with it attempts are made to create systems of meaning for members of society'.

For many, in addition to these factors, work reinforces a person's **concept of self** (how we regard ourselves, as shown by answering the question 'Tell me about yourself' with 'Well, I am a teacher …'). People also have a desire to **conform**, be **obedient** and are influenced by **group pressure**. They also have a desire for social contact and work provides this, hence many affluent people still remain in work. Work also allows a person to achieve what Maslow called **self-actualization** or achieving something that a person really wants to achieve.

Conformity and obedience

While it might be difficult, in most developed societies it is possible to live without working. Even though low levels of social security motivate people to gain employment, other factors are at play. Humans are open to suggestibility (contagious behaviour) as seen by people mirroring each other's body language, purchasing a new car because a neighbour has or following a fashion. Suggestibility has been tested under experimental conditions. Soloman Asch (1955) proposed that suggestibility can overcome a person's acknowledgement of what he or she knows to be the truth. Asch devised a simple test in which lines of various lengths were shown to a group who all stated which was the longest line. One member of the group, unaware that the others were working for Asch, agreed that an obviously short line was the longest when his colleagues unanimously stated that it was. Such is the power of suggestibility and it affects people in all aspects of life:

- Adverts show ideal families and homes.
- Magazines show beautiful, successful people.
- Society promotes successful people as role models.

All of these influences both consciously and subconsciously encourage people to gain employment and seek advancement in order to be like those role models.

Normative social influence

In addition to suggestibility, people are sensitive to social norms (understood rules for accepted and expected behaviour). Working, rather than living on state handouts, is generally regarded as the social norm in developed societies and work from an early age is the norm in many developing cultures. To stray from these norms would expose someone to negative social opinion and most people prefer not to suffer that.

Social norms have changed over time. The Ancient Greeks regarded the most desirable life as one of leisure and pursuit of pleasure. Work was regarded as demeaning and reserved for the lowest social orders and in particular to slaves. Slavery was the social device that enabled the Greeks to maintain their view of work as something to be avoided by a full human being (Watson, 1987).

The Romans tended to have the same attitude to work as the Greeks, while early Christians saw that work could divert people from sinful thoughts. With the Reformation came the notion that a person's work was his or her calling and with the growth of capitalism, work became an essential prerequisite of personal and social advancement of prestige, virtue and self fulfilment (Watson, 1987). More recently, a culture of trying to achieve success meant less successful people were often regarded as failures.

Social facilitation

Norman Triplett (1898) noticed that cyclists raced faster when they competed against each other rather than against the clock. To test this hypothesis he gave teenagers fishing reels and asked them to wind them in as quickly as possible. When doing this in pairs, they wound faster than when alone. Towler (1986) found similar effects in drivers, where they move away from green traffic lights, 15 per cent faster if there are other cars alongside them.

This greater performance in front of others is known as **social facilitation** and this may explain why people compete to get good jobs and certainly why working with others is likely to result in greater productivity than as individuals.

There are negative aspects to social influence, suggestibility and obedience and this can be seen most graphically in the experiments of Stanley Milgram (1974). Milgram showed that people were perfectly willing to 'electrocute' another test subject whenever they got questions wrong, simply because they had been instructed to do so (the electricity wasn't real but the screams were!). Browning (1992) records one of the many atrocities carried out during World War II. In Jozfow, Poland, 500 middle-aged reserve police officers were ordered to kill 1500 helpless women and children. The police reserves were given the option of not being involved but only 15 declined, despite the fact that many of the victims were known to them.

Commentary

Less graphic examples can been seen in the workplace.
- Deliberately keeping production levels low, with punishments given to those who work too hard.
- Them and us cultures being maintained by the workforce even when management tries to develop a more participative culture.
- Cultures of harassment and racial bias continue even when individuals do not normally harbour these feelings (often called institutional racism or sexism).

Work in different cultures

Most texts covering the role of work cover western societies only and therefore it would be easy to assume that the attitude is the same in all cultures. However, this is not the case.

In China, jobs are still found by the state if a job is not held with a commercial company. The culture is still primarily a state-run communist one, and only recently are people becoming more commercially and customer orientated. Young educated Chinese are increasingly wanting careers gained through ability rather than government appointment. Birth control is regulated by the government due to the massive population. Parents must seek permission to have children and most will only be allowed to have one child. There are accounts of shopfloor supervisors recording the menstrual cycles of female employees, so they can identify if they appear to be having an unplanned pregnancy.

In Japan, work is regarded as essential with 'gambare' (persistence and the will to endure) regarded as the norm, as seen in children's stories where characters better themselves. This was also shown in a survey of executives' favourite words. In Europe their favourites were 'love, family and fun', whereas in Japan they were 'effort, persistence and thank you'. At Mazda's factory in Hiroshima, children's drawings can be seen on the walls with gambare slogans, to remind their fathers to work hard and diligently.

'Kaizen', or 'ongoing improvement', is also part of Japanese culture, yet has to be imposed in most western organizations in an effort to improve quality and efficiency. In Japan, the Kaizen philosophy extends beyond work and into the home and personal relationships. The belief that improvement is unending is clearly shown in a traditional Japanese motto: 'If a man has not been seen for three days, his friends should take a good look at him to see what changes have befallen him'.

Education is highly encouraged in Japan and enduring challenges is seen as character building and an integral part of achieving the goal itself. Traditionally, once someone joined an employer he or she was employed for life. However, recent downturns in the Japanese economy have brought about redundancies, seriously affecting the psychological contracts of workers.

In under-developed countries, particularly where education is not compulsory or prolific, working from an early age is the norm, partly due to the subsistence level of living and partly due to social norms. In rural India women do much of the work even from an early age. A study showed that girls spend 60 per cent of their time doing household work while boys spend 60 per cent of their time playing.

Commentary

While studies have shown that motivational needs are similar around the globe, clearly, there are cultural differences that would influence the manner in which people are managed. The notion of gambare, while instilled from childhood in Japan, is not in most other cultures, and the notion of monitoring females' menstrual cycles would definitely not go down too well outside of China!

Answer this before reading on:

A boy is badly injured as he runs across the road to his father, who has come to pick him up from school. The paramedics arrive and rush the boy and his father to the hospital where it is decided that the boy needs emergency surgery. In the operating theatre the surgeon pulls back the covers and in a state of shock says, 'I cannot operate on this boy, he is my son.'

What is the relationship between the boy and the surgeon?

Social roles

In addition to certain norms that society reinforces, there are roles that tend to be associated with gender. In the question above, most people, particularly if they haven't been prompted by the topic of gender roles, get very confused and try to find ways that the surgeon could be the father or stepfather. The answer is, of course, that the surgeon was the boy's mother, yet very few people (male or female) think of this as they automatically associate the role of surgeon as a male preserve. The same view tends to be held about pilots, engineers and, in particular, managers.

Catering, cleaning, retail, nursing, and customer service roles are generally female dominated and also lower paid than equivalent 'male' roles. This example of social and gender norming occurs early on in life when children are encouraged to act and play differently depending upon their sex. At school, girls have traditionally followed academic routes that encouraged the development of clerical, catering, teaching, caring skills or the arts, whereas boys have tended to be steered towards sciences and subjects that support the professions or skilled manual roles. As a result, far fewer females have the req-

uisite qualifications to undertake certain higher education courses or apply for jobs, even if they had the confidence to overcome the notion that their choice was not a 'normal' one for a female. This is shown dramatically in figures from the USA where women make up 3 per cent of top executives, 4 per cent of the Marine corps, 97 per cent of nurses, and 99 per cent of secretaries.

The roles of women vary around the world in this regard. For instance, women fill 48 per cent of managerial positions in Switzerland, 28 per cent in Austria, 17 per cent in the USA, 3 per cent in Ghana and 2 per cent in South Korea (Triandes, 1994).

In the UK, males still dominate the world of management particularly at senior levels as shown in Figure 2.1.

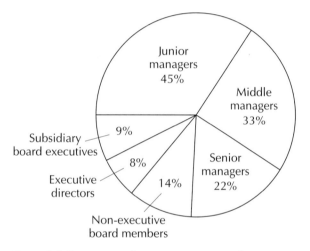

Figure 2.1: Percentage of women managers in the private sector in the UK

The male breadwinner

The male is traditionally regarded as the 'bread winner' or main income source in most western societies, whereas in many developing cultures, the men relax while the women do the bulk of the work. For a man to have a 'lesser' career role and income than his female partner is often regarded with some amusement and surprise, as it is still far more common for the woman to follow her partner as his career develops. When women deviate from this social convention it can make men feel anxious or be viewed as weird (Green and Sandos, 1983).

Evolutionists would explain this in terms of the male having originally been the hunter (although we don't know this for sure) and the female the carer of the children. Even today, society tends to preserve the notion that women should be the primary child carers and many still frown upon women who return to work straight after childbirth, particularly if it was not necessary economically. There is some evidence that young people are increasingly finding the notion more acceptable than, for instance, their parents may have.

Career choice

The choice of career is not only influenced by gender and society's expectations. Often people follow their parents into similar roles or industries and it can be a big wrench to step away from such a destiny. Roberts (1975) stressed that for many individuals, entry to work is a matter of:

'fitting oneself into whatever jobs are available given the qualifications which one's class and educational background has enabled one to gain'.

Watson (1987) proposes a model that allows for both objective and subjective factors (see Figure 2.2). Objectively, the individual has resources such as money, knowledge and strength while subjectively he or she also has motives, interests and expectations such as achieving power. Both of these factors are influenced by structural settings such as family background and occupational structure and the prevailing job market.

Career motivations are increasingly being assessed from an early age. School children are often given motivation questionnaires by careers advisers, with varying degrees of success due to the still forming personality and motives of many adolescents. For adults already in employment, motivation surveys offer a more practical and revealing method of guiding future career direction and progression (see p. 45).

Commentary

Motivation surveys are an excellent way of identifying what people prefer to have in the job role that will 'give them a buzz', but what is that 'buzz' they get, and why does it often fade over time?

Motivation like intelligence, is very difficult to define.

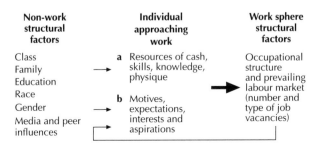

Non-work structural factors	Individual approaching work	Work sphere structural factors
Class Family Education Race Gender Media and peer influences	**a** Resources of cash, skills, knowledge, physique **b** Motives, expectations, interests and aspirations	Occupational structure and prevailing labour market (number and type of job vacancies)

Figure 2.2: Factors influencing the individual's approach to work, based on Watson (1987)

Most definitions revolve around a need or desire that energizes behaviour towards a goal. Essentially, it concerns why people act and think in the way they do. For instance, why are you reading this book? What motivated to you to buy and read it? The answer to this question will vary depending upon which school of psychological thought you ascribe to.

Psychological explanations of motivation

Freud, a psychoanalytic psychologist, would attempt to identify unconscious motives and wishes. Behaviourists such as Skinner would look for reinforcement. Maslow, a humanist, would relate behaviour to self-actualization. A neurobiological psychologist would look for processes taking place in the nervous and endocrine systems. A cognitive psychologist would relate the way individuals think to the way they act, and Jung would relate behaviour to aspects of personality.

Commentary

With such a wealth of viewpoints, psychologists have attempted to combine theories in order to show better the various potential reasons for motivation to act in certain ways. However, to understand these combined models it is important to see the foundations of the theories they are comprised of. The next section examines the main theories of motivation.

Instinct theory

As the evolutionary theories of Darwin gained greater popularity at the start of the last century, behaviour was often explained in terms of instincts. An instinct is a:

'complex behaviour that has a fixed pattern throughout the species and cannot be taught' (Tinbergen, 1951).

Such behaviours are clearly apparent in animals such as imprinting and homing, while humans display instinctive drives for suckling, feeding, reproduction and protection of the young.

Commentary

Instinct and evolutionary theories are only useful to an extent in explaining workplace motivations, particularly as a lot of work in this field was simply orientated towards labelling instincts. McDougal (1928) identified 800 separate instincts but explained none of them.

Drive reduction theory

Woodworth (1928) first used the word 'drive' rather than instinct when comparing human behaviour to the way a machine works. The analogy being that a machine is passive or stationary until power makes it go. The aim of drive reduction is **homeostasis**, the maintenance of a steady internal state. **Homeostatic drive theory** (Cannon, 1929) can be seen in the way in which the body keeps a chemical equilibrium without the human having to think about it most of the time. For instance, people sweat when hot, without having to think about it, yet if an imbalance such as hunger, thirst or suffocation occurs, this causes humans to be driven (motivated) to find food, water or air. In turn, it is possible to see how this encourages learning. As drives (e.g. hunger) reduce after an action (e.g. eating), people learn the effect that action has on them and this reinforces that action, so that it is repeated when required (when hungry, you eat).'

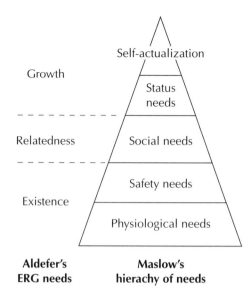

Figure 2.3: Maslow's hierarchy of needs and Aldefer's ERG needs

Commentary

So why is this a drive *reduction* theory as opposed to just a drive theory? The reason is that the effect of fulfilling the need caused by homeostatic drive (eating, drinking) leads to those organs no longer requiring food or water for now, so the drive is reduced.

Arousal theory

Instinct theories cannot explain why some people have to climb mountains or become fans of certain types of music. Arousal theory attempts to explain this by stating that humans have an inherent need to experience stimulation, without it they feel bored or look elsewhere for some other means of arousal. This is particularly relevant to workers who carry out repetitive, low-skill, low-cognitive tasks day after day. Boredom causes high job turnover as employees seek stimulation elsewhere. This effect can be alleviated by job rotation and job enrichment (see p. 39).

Incentive theory

In addition to being pushed by their needs, people also experience incentives every day – the smell of a nice meal, the sight of someone attractive, the lure of that new car advertised on TV. When incentives and needs combine, a high level of drive or motivation exists and behaviour is likely to be altered.

Hierarchy of motives

One of the most frequently quoted motivational models was proposed by sociologist Abraham Maslow in 1970 (see Figure 2.3). Maslow maintained that some needs are more important than

others, hence the drive to fulfil them will be greater.

Maslow maintained that once individuals' physiological needs are met, for instance a job that allows them to feed, clothe and shelter their family, then they will be motivated to look for security of employment, medical insurance and pensions to ensure their safety needs. Once all of the basic needs are met, they will look for social needs such as affection and a sense of belonging, with an eventual aim of getting a job that allows them to have all of the other needs satisfied but also to be able to do what they have always wanted to do. This is called self-actualization. Examples might be to travel, to paint or to write a book on psychology, yet according to Maslow, this is only a main motive, once the other needs are fulfilled.

Commentary

It is the concept that one need starts when another is fulfilled that has led to much criticism of Maslow's model (despite this, it is taught on nearly every management course!). Some people choose to live near the poverty line so that they can fulfil their ideal jobs, which goes against Maslow's hierarchy of needs. Equally, if someone is made redundant from a high status job, he or she would probably take any job, even if before he or she was motivated mainly by esteem.

Aldefer (1972) built on Maslow's model by proposing three groups of needs: existence, relatedness and growth. Unlike Maslow's hierarchical model, Aldefer proposed a sliding scale that moves depending upon the circumstances. Sugarman (1995) clarified the characteristics of self-actualization (see Figure 2.4) as relatively few people achieve this level and therefore it is often difficult to imagine.

1 *Perceives people and events accurately*, without undue interference from their own preconceptions

2 *Accepts self and others*, including imperfections, but seeks improvement where possible

3 *Is spontaneous*, especially in own thoughts and feelings

4 *Focuses on problems outside self*, rather than being insecure and introspective

5 *Is detached*, so that not unduly thrown off course by awkward events

6 *Is autonomous*, and remains true to self despite pressure to conform

7 *Appreciates good and beautiful things*, even if they are familiar

8 *Has peak experiences* of intense positive emotions of a sometimes mystic quality

9 *Has close relationships*, but only with a few carefully chosen people

10 *Respects others*, avoids making fun of people and evaluates them according to their inner qualities rather than race or social class

11 *Has firm moral standards*, and sense of right and wrong, though these may be different from many other people's

12 *Is creative*: this is perhaps the most fundamental aspect of self-actualization, and is seen as the result of the other aspects listed above. By being open-minded and open to own experience, the self-actualizing person sees things in novel ways and can draw novel conclusions from established information

Figure 2.4: Characteristics of someone who is self-actualizing

Figure 2.5: Analysing ambiguous pictures can provide an insight into someone's level of achievement motivation

Achievement needs

McClelland (1961) proposed a needs theory of work motivation based around the need for achievement, which he maintained was essential for economic prosperity. Cassidy and Lynn (1989) identified six components to the need for achievement:

- Work ethic – the motivation to achieve based on the belief that performance is good in itself.
- Pursuit of excellence – a desire to perform to the best of one's ability.
- Status aspiration – a desire to climb the status hierarchy and dominate others.
- Competitiveness – a desire to compete with others and win.
- Acquisitiveness – wanting to acquire money.
- Mastery – competitiveness against certain standards rather than against others.

While most people may be motivated by the need to achieve, how strong is that need? McClelland and Atkinson (1953) sought to measure achievement need by asking people to write stories in line with what they saw in a picture such as Figure 2.5.

If they wrote stories that included references to the boy daydreaming about being heroic or walking on the moon for instance, then they would have been said to have shown a high level of achievement motivation. Such people tend to persist with tasks that are difficult (Cooper, 1983), while those with low achievement needs tend to select easy tasks or those with which they are likely to fail (Green, 1984) and are less likely to complete a college course or have a successful marriage (McCall, 1994). Achievement needs are routinely assessed in modern personality questionnaires. In the OPQ32 report on p. 19, achievement needs would be shown by the 'Dynamism' group of behaviours.

Commentary

Our desire for achievement is always going to be tempered by the realistic expectation of that dream coming true. The author has two distinct dreams, namely to travel into space and also to marry Shania Twain, however despite these desires, I have not enrolled in space camp nor started stalking Shania! The reason being that it is extremely unlikely that I will travel into space and opinions vary as to my marriage chances! This is an example of expectancy theory and is the same reason why many people do not go for certain jobs, or attempt certain projects.

Expectancy theory was first put forward by Vroom (1964) who proposed three factors that affect people's motivation to act in certain ways. The first he called **expectancy** (if I were to do this, would I be able to do it?), the second **instrumentality** (assuming that I could do it, would I achieve the result I want?) and the third **valence** (how much do I want that result?). Vroom proposed that it is possible to calculate the level of motivation by giving a rating to each of the three factors and multiplying them. If any of the factors are rated at zero, such as the likelihood of succeeding, then the motivation score would also be zero.

Commentary

This has important implications for managers who attempt to motivate a workforce, particularly if they use incentives. If a target is set very high (low expectancy), motivation is going to be low, even if the desire (valence) for the bonus is very high. Interestingly, the seemingly impossible chance of winning the lottery, does not seem to stop people trying!

Studies have also shown that both **intrinsic** (part of the job itself) and **extrinsic** factors (pay, conditions, etc.) will be borne in mind by individuals when they perceive the overall appeal of the reward on offer. Porter and Lawler (1968) refined the expectancy theory accordingly and placed it in an organizational context, with practical concerns included too, thereby increasing the number of variables that individuals would consider when deciding the probability that their actions would succeed (see Figure 2.6).

Intrinsic and extrinsic rewards were highlighted by **Fredrick Herzberg** as being key determinates of motivation. Herzberg studied engineers and accountants and has since carried out 16 other investigations using a wide variety of populations to identify the factors involved in producing job satisfaction and motivation. Herzberg referred to extrinsic factors as **hygiene factors** from the analogy that keeping things clean doesn't make people well but by not doing it, people may get ill. Similarly, factors outside of the job itself such as pay, working conditions, perks and holidays will not make people more motivated to work harder but by taking them away (or reducing them) the people will become demotivated.

Commentary

The idea that money is in fact a demotivator rather than a motivator, often causes some confusion and is probably best 'proved' with an example. If someone was given a 20 per cent pay increase, for a short time he or she would probably be very highly motivated. After a while,

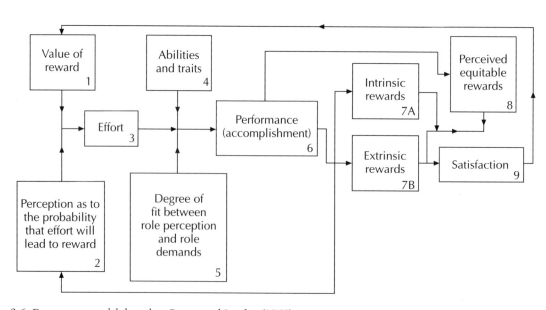

Figure 2.6: Expectancy model, based on Porter and Lawler (1968)

Table 2.1: Principles of vertical job loading (job enrichment)

Principle	Motivators involved
A Removing some controls while maintaining accountability	Responsibility and personal achievement
B Increasing the accountability of individuals for own work	Responsibility and recognition
C Giving a person a complete natural unit of work (module, division, area and so on)	Responsibility, achievement and recognition
D Granting additional authority to employees in their activity; job freedom	Responsibility, achievement and recognition
E Making periodic reports directly available to the workers themselves rather than to supervisors	Internal recognition
F Introducing new and more difficult tasks not previously handled	Growth and learning
G Assigning individuals specific or specialized tasks, enabling them to become experts	Responsibility, growth, and advancement

Reprinted by permission of *Harvard Business Review*, from 'One More Time: How do you motivate employees?' by Frederick Herzberg, September October 1987. Copyright © 1987 by the President and Fellows of Harvard College; all rights reserved.

the money would become a normal factor of the job and the motivating effect, if any, would go. If, however, the person's salary was cut by 20 per cent he or she would be very demotivated and this feeling would last for a long time.

Intrinsic motivators are factors such as the job itself, the enjoyment gained, the challenge, the sense of status, self worth and social contact. Herzberg proposed that to motivate employees it is essential to ensure that **extrinsic motivators** are addressed and do not decline and that managers should concentrate on **job enrichment** to build on the **intrinsic motivators**.

Herzberg suggests the approach to job enrichment or vertical job loading shown in Table 2.1.

Commentary

This counters the preference among many managers to give what Herzberg calls KITA (Kick In The Arse.) While this might seem an obvious way of getting someone to do something, it is not motivating that individual. Herzberg's work has become standard reading, leading to many jobs being enriched. Unfortunately, many managers simply add more responsibilities (job enlargement) rather than enriching them, or managers rotate work around workers, which simply relieves boredom.

Cross-cultural differences.

Herzberg has assessed the motivating and demotivating characteristics of hygiene (extrinsic) factors and motivating (intrinsic) factors of work in a number of countries, showing that the influence of both seems to be common (see Figure 2.7).

Commentary

In Figure 2.7 the top bar for each country shows the proportion of factors thought to dissatisfy or demotivate. The lower bar shows the proportion of hygiene/motivator factors involved in satisfying people. Overall, it offers a resounding endorsement that extrinsic factors contribute most to dissatisfying people and intrinsic to satisfying them (see RLA 3).

Real Life Application 3:

NHS faces worst staffing crisis in 26 years

The NHS is facing the worst nursing shortages in 26 years with a record 17 000 vacancies unfilled. According to a report by the Kings Fund, a leading health think tank, increasing numbers of nurses, disillusioned by poor pay and inadequate hospitals are leaving the profession. In the interviews held with nurses they complained of inflexible working times, lack of affordable housing, poor career progression and insecurity. Nurses are also five times as likely to be attacked at work than the general public. Other nurses complained of 'pathetic and embarrassing' shortages of basic items such as pillows and pyjamas.

Adverts by unions campaigning for better conditions have also had a negative effect. One poster said: 'When you pay peanuts what do you get? A caring, competent and undervalued woman.'

Article adapted from 'NHS faces worst staff crisis in 26 years' by Rosie Waterhouse in *The Sunday Times*, 9 July 2000.

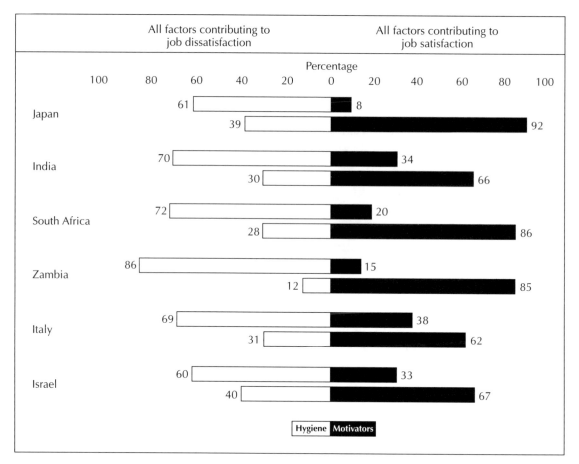

Figure 2.7: How the hygiene motivator factors affect job attitudes in six countries

Reprinted by permission of *Harvard Business Review*, from 'One More Time: How do you motivate employees?' by Frederick Herzberg, September October 1987. Copyright © 1987 by the President and Fellows of Harvard College; all rights reserved.

Summary

- The report links staff shortages with extrinsic demotivators such as pay and working conditions. Lack of career progression and an inability to perform properly due to lack of resources is also cited.
- An advert designed to highlight the issue, possibly helped to reinforce the image that nurses are underpaid and undervalued. Note also that even the trade union indicates that nurses are women (see p. 34 on social roles).

Questions

1 What steps could be made to address the issues raised in the article?

2 What would be the psychological effects of these actions?

Herzberg is not alone in maintaining that extrinsic factors, particularly pay, do not motivate. Pfeffer (1998) states that pay 'in reality, undermines performance' while Kohn (1993) contends that:

'incentive plans must fail because they are based on a patently inadequate theory of motivation'.

Rosabeth Moss Kanter (1979) highlights how pay tends to reflect where a job ranks in the corporate hierarchy as opposed to the work that gets done. This system, she proposes, is now under attack with a big push back on those perceived to be 'fat cats' and earning too much for the job they are doing.

Goldthorpe and Lockwood (1968) add another element to the debate over intrinsic and extrinsic motivators in their studies of well-paid car production workers. They found that there was no relationship between the levels of job satisfaction and their decision to remain employed there doing the jobs they were doing. In their studies, however, the level of pay was the most commonly cited reason for staying with an employer. So, if extrinsic factors were not a major influence on job satisfaction or motivation, then surely intrinsic factors must have been? Not necessarily, say Goldthorpe and Lockwood; they found at Vauxhall that many shopfloor workers had little or no intrinsic rewards, yet were not dissatisfied. They appear to have accepted that when they joined they had 'an instrumental orientation to work'.

Commentary

While Goldthorpe and Lockwood's work has been criticized for placing too much emphasis on people's initial choice of career, it is a very interesting notion that people who are reasonably well paid might receive little motivation (intrinsic or extrinsic), yet work hard due to an inherent desire to work and an acceptance when they started that they would receive little motivation.

Equity theory

Equity theory of motivation is similar to expectancy theory in that it suggests a cognitive process is at play governing whether an individual puts effort in or not. In this instance the effort is determined by whether the person feels he or she is being treated fairly. Adams (1963) states:

'if we perceive our input as justifying a larger output or if on a comparative basis we feel we are unfairly treated, feelings of inequity can arise'.

Adams suggests six courses of action that are open to people to reduce this inequity:

- Inputs such as effort could be reduced.
- Outputs such as pay could increase.
- Perceptions of self could be modified. They could alter their perception of how much they are valued.
- Modification of the perceptions of others with

whom comparisons are made, i.e. they may decide that the other person must actually be working harder, hence their higher pay.
- The person with whom a comparison is made is no longer used, instead they compare themselves with someone else.
- Leave the situation, for instance resign.

Goal setting theory

Ed Locke pioneered an approach to motivation in the 1960s that centred on setting objectives or goals for an individual. Others have built on his theories, so much so that over half the academic articles on motivation published in the 1980s were on goal setting theory. Current goal setting theory involves the attitudes to a goal being influenced by incentives (such as money), self-perception of own ability and the manner in which the goals were set (see Figure 2.8).

In turn, the characteristics of the goal and the attitudes towards it determine what action or behavioural strategy the person will select. This leads to a performance, within the limits of the person's ability and in light of how it turns out, future performance is refined. Reviews by Locke *et al* (1981) and Mento *et al* (1987) substantiate the goal setting theory, particularly for difficult goals where the person was involved in setting the goals, also for specific goals and when feedback is given. Austin and Bobko (1985) though identified four areas in which goal setting theory had not been tested:

- where the goal reflected quality
- multiple competing goals
- goals for teams
- goals outside of laboratory conditions.

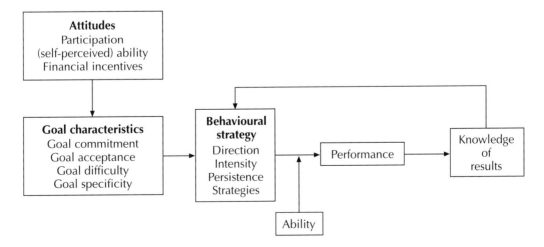

Figure 2.8: Goal setting theory

Despite these caveats, goal setting theory is the most consistently supported theory in occupational psychology, in fact 90 per cent of all laboratory and field research studies produced supporting results (Locke *et al*, 1981).

The theories of motivation put forward so far indicate that people are generally motivated by a common set of factors, including personality but to varying degrees. McGregor (1960) went one step further and broadly categorized people into two distinct groups when it comes to motivation to work. Schein later added a third group in 1980. The three approaches to work are called **Theory X**, **Theory Y** and **Social**.

Theory X people maintain that other people cannot be trusted as they believe them to be irrational, unreliable and inherently lazy. As a result, they should be controlled through financial incentives and punishments.

Theory Y people are looking for independence, self-development and creativity in their work. They look ahead and are able to adapt to new situations. They are fundamentally responsible beings who will work to the good of the company, if they are treated with this in mind.

Social (Schein, 1980) states that a person's behaviour is mainly influenced by social interactions which influence his or her sense of identity and belonging at work. People look for meaningful relationships and are more responsive to the expectations of others than they are to financial incentives.

It has been proposed that most managers lean towards one of these viewpoints and as a result the way in which they try to motivate their staff will vary. This is explored further in Chapter 3.

Integration of motivation theories

Mitchel (1982) suggested that more attention should be paid to integrating the numerous perspectives on motivation. One such model was proposed by Klein (1989) (see Figure 2.9).

Commentary

While Klein's model looks complicated it is both simple and useful, if you follow it through:

Step 1 – the goal that triggers the behaviour.

Steps 2 and 3 – the behaviour happens.

Steps 4 and 5 – feedback on that behaviour is required and is compared to the original goal.

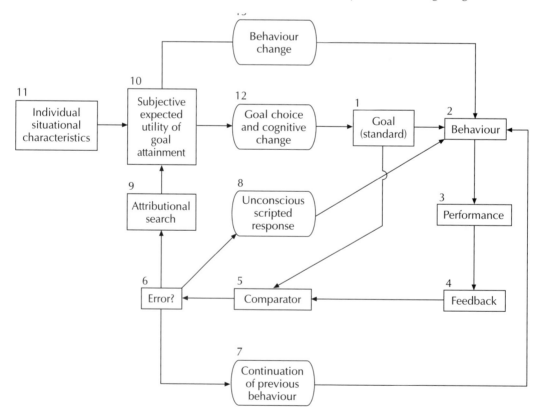

Figure 2.9: Integrated model of work motivation, based on Klein (1989)

Steps 6 and 7 – were the results what was expected?

Steps 8 and 9 – if the results were not as expected, then the person could undertake a scripted response (doing what you know you do in certain situations, e.g. if you bump into someone, you say 'Sorry, are you all right?') or the person could find out why it didn't achieve what was expected.

Step 10 – out of the search for reasons comes a re-evaluation of the original goal.

Step 11 – the individual's needs, abilities and the situation influence this re-evaluation.

Step 12 – the goal may change as a result of this re-evaluation.

Step 13 – the behaviour may change as a result.

Practical applications

The desire to motivate employees has been a strong influence on managers for hundreds of years because of the belief that a motivated employee will work more effectively. Early last century, major employers such as AT&T and the Rockefeller Foundation sponsored considerable research into how motivation theories could be used to make employees more effective.

Elton Mayo with his study of female workers in Hawthorne, Chicago, found that altering the manner of supervision and giving more control to employees was highly motivational (see Key Study 3). However, when Mayo carried out a subsequent study of men in the bank wiring room of a factory that made equipment for telephone exchanges, he found that while productivity initially increased, those working harder were punished by the rest of the group. As a result of this peer pressure an unofficial output level was maintained, regardless of any motivational changes.

The challenge of enriching routine jobs

As theories of job enrichment spread through the world of management thinking, managers attempted to enrich the roles of those working for them. Many, however, as Herzberg noted, simply added more work to existing levels, which actually demotivated employees. The problem is most pronounced in routine jobs that are unskilled and do not involve much thinking. One solution is to rotate employees around different jobs but all this does is relieve boredom. Drawing upon the numerous references to social contact being a motivator (e.g. Maslow) production lines started to be organized so that workers faced each other and could converse. Assembly plants became organized into cells where

---

KEY STUDY 3

Researcher:	Elton Mayo, sponsored by AT&T (1924–32)
Aims:	To increase productivity at AT&T's Western Electric Factory in Hawthorne, Chicago, 1924–32.
Method:	Mayo believed that altering the working conditions would affect productivity. He improved lighting, and introduced rest breaks.
Results:	Productivity increased with each change. However, it also increased when he returned conditions to the original state. Mayo segregated five female employees to experiment further and the same results occurred.
Conclusions:	Mayo having interviewed the employees found that it was not the change in working conditions that motivated them but the fact that they were being taken notice of and that they were being studied, rather than supervised. Being part of the experiment they felt united and a team. This became known as the **Hawthorne effect** and influenced the style of supervision worldwide.
Critics:	Subsequent studies of the original notes reveal that Mayo may have popularized his findings and that in reality the results were inconclusive. The published results also ignored the workers' views that they were motivated by improving extrinsic factors (Gillespie, 1991).

---

three or four could converse and benefit from a level of social facilitation (subconscious competitiveness).

This principle led on to cellular manufacturing where machines were arranged not in rows but around one or two employees (see Figure 2.10). Instead of one person operating one machine and waiting while it completes its process, a few employees would move around each machine whenever it needed attention, thereby keeping them busy all the time and making them multi-skilled.

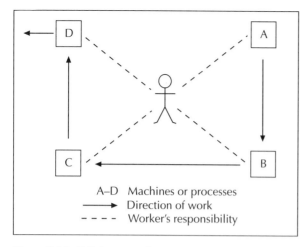

Figure 2.10: Cellular manufacturing

Other changes that have increasingly appeared as a result of motivation theory are involving employees more in decision making and where possible **empowering** them to make decisions and be accountable for their results. This motivates many people by increasing the cognitive side of the role and boosting their esteem.

Better communication has also been found to motivate employees not simply because they have more information to make decisions but because they feel more trusted and involved in the business.

These factors and others were highlighted by Bill Byham in his best-selling book *Zapp* (1991) and he has subsequently founded a multimillion-dollar global training company, DDI, which bases its training on what Byham calls 'Zappers'. In addition, Byham identified 'Sappers' or demotivators. Byham and his researchers have found that these apply in all developed cultures albeit that the relative importance of each may vary (see Table 2.2).

Table 2.2: Zappers (motivators) and Sappers (demotivators)

Zappers	Sappers
Maintain or enhance self-esteem	Meaningless, repetitive work
Listen and respond with empathy	Lack of trust
Share thoughts, feelings and rationale	No input on decisions
Ask for help and encourage involvement	Someone solving problems for you
Provide support without removing responsibility for action	Not getting feedback or recognition
	Everyone treated like interchangeable parts

Commentary

Managers are generally seeking to improve the motivation of their workforce, yet to do so assumes that:
- they are not already as motivated as they could be in the jobs they are doing
- increased motivation leads to greater performance
- the employees are not motivated by the work at all (they may be in the wrong career)
- what the manager feels is motivating to themselves applies to others. A difference in motivations exists between individuals particularly if they are at different stages in their life.

Because motivational needs vary, motivation surveys are increasingly being used to identify the motivators. One such example is the SHL Motivation Questionnaire (MQ) which can be used by British Psychological Society Level B holders (see p. 45). It is based on the notion that motivation is influenced by the characteristics of the person, the job and the organization in which he or she works. It therefore tries to identify the difference in the factors which energize, direct and sustain behaviour in the workplace. There are 144 questions covering 19 motivational influences that are grouped into four broad groups (see Figure 2.11). Users rank statements on a scale from 'Greatly reduces my motivation to work' through to 'Greatly increases my motivation to work'.

Examples of SHL MQ statements include the following:

- The need to be constantly on the go in the job.
- Having little contact with colleagues.
- Being free to organize own work.

Used in the same way as personality questionnaires, an MQ can help to guide individuals towards a certain career path, help identify what's lacking from their current role and identify trends within a team that might allow the manager to better motivate them.

Reward systems

Rewards are extrinsic motivators (see p. 38) and are also **positive reinforcers**. **Behaviourists** such as **Skinner** maintain that regular reminders that certain actions provide a reward, cause changes in behaviour.

Rewards include:

- salary increases
- share options

Level of activity – Invests energy readily. Thrives on time pressure. Always on the go. Pushes to get things done

Achievement – Needs to achieve targets. Strives to overcome difficult challenges

Competition – Tries to do better than others. Comparison often spurs performance

Fear of failure – Needs to succeed to maintain self-esteem. Prospect of failure spurs activity

Power – Needs scope to influence and exercise authority. Demotivated when not given responsibility

Immersion – Thrives on feeling involved. Invests energy in job. Prepared to work extended hours

Commercial outlook – Likes creating wealth and profits. Demotivated when work not linked with cash value

ENERGY AND DYNAMISM

Affiliation – Thrives on meeting people, harmonious team work and helping others

Recognition – Likes good work to be noticed and achievements recognized. Becomes demotivated without support

Personal principles – Needs to feel that the organization's work is sound. Demotivated when asked to compromise ethical standards

Ease and security – Needs to feel secure about job and position. Does not easily tolerate unpleasant conditions

Personal growth – Motivated by work which provides opportunities for development, and acquisition of new skills

SYNERGY

Interest – Values stimulating, varied or creative work. Demotivated to too many run-of-the-mill tasks

Flexibility – Favours a fluid environment without imposed structure. High tolerance of ambiguity

Autonomy – Needs to work independently, organize own approach. Demotivated by close supervision

INTRINSIC

Material reward – Links salary, perks and bonuses to success. Demotivated when remuneration is perceived as unfair or poor

Progression – Career progress and just advancement are motivating. Slow promotion is demotivating

Status – Concerned with position and status. Demotivated by lack of respect from others

EXTRINSIC

Figure 2.11: Motivational factors assessed by the Saville and Holdsworth Motivation Questionnaire, SHL Group PLC

- discount cards
- leisure clubs
- bonuses
- promotions.

The fair distribution of such rewards is open to bias and subjectivity for the same reasons listed on p.00. Performance appraisals are the most common method of identifying what type of level of reward is to be given. The main purpose of a reward system is to attract, retain and motivate qualified employees. Moorhead and Griffin (1992) listed three factors that should be borne in mind with any reward system. It should provide:

- fair and equitable rewards
- a recognition of the importance of each employee's contribution to the organization, although in practice it is difficult to measure these contributions in a tangible way
- the compensation (reward) package on offer must be competitive in the external employment market in order to attract and retain competent staff.

Pay

Pay, salary or compensation as it is referred to in the US, is the most common method of rewarding employees. A traditional approach to pay, used far less now, was piece rate where the level of pay reflected the output of that person. This made it particularly suitable for production or administrative processes. For example:

10 widgets per day = £50, i.e. £5 paid per widget

10 widgets = the average amount a good employee can realistically make in a day

Over 10 widgets per day earns the worker £10 per widget.

Thus piece rate should ensure that employees

produce at least ten units per day as less than that would make the reward too low and more than ten would mean a significant improvement in earnings.

Paying commission or on-target earnings is simply another form of piece rate and is still used in sales environments. It works by paying a low basic salary, which is topped up every time a sale is made.

Commentary

There were many problems with piece rate even though, if levels and rewards were set correctly, it could produce high productivity.

Firstly, it is difficult to set the optimum rate, particularly as people get more effective at carrying out tasks with practice, therefore targets get easier. In addition, employees can cut corners and exceed their targets, which might lower quality or put them at risk due to ignoring health and safety rules. If the rate per unit is set too high individual employees may stop producing once they feel that they have earned sufficient for the day. Part of the psychological contract concerns what the employee feels is a fair day's work and management often tries to increase this through altering the piece rate. Due to the individual nature of piece rate, colleagues would have no incentive to help others.

Piece rate is far less common now because of these problems.

Basic pay

Now normally paid monthly direct into a bank account, pay was traditionally in cash and given in a little brown packet, hence the phrase 'pay packet'. Cash was the preferred option for male workers as it meant their wives didn't know how much they were earning!

Lawler (1981) highlighted how it is possible to use pay as a reward mechanism:

- **Importance** – pay is important to most people.
- **Flexibility** – pay can be altered to reflect performance or promotion.
- **Frequency** – pay can be used frequently and still retain most of its worth.
- **Visibility** – the link between pay and performance can be made explicit.

Commentary

While Lawler shows how pay can be used to reward and reinforce behaviours (people learn that certain actions bring about reward, so they then do them more – punishment has the opposite effect), it is rarely used effectively because it tends not to vary in size or frequency.

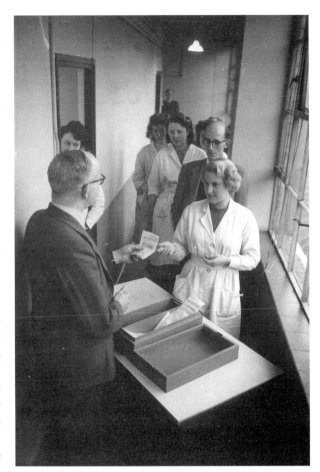

Workers queue to receive their pay packet

Therefore 'pay packets' are difficult to relate to how someone performed that month. If, however, after each output (e.g. a sale) individual employees were immediately given cash, in front of their colleagues, it would provide a far more reinforcing effect, i.e. that they should repeat that behaviour (at least until sufficient money had been earned). Lawler's studies found that only 22 per cent of workers actually had faith that their pay and performance were linked properly (Lawler, 1984).

Performance-related pay

To make the link between performance and pay more explicit and therefore make pay more motivating and reinforcing, performance-related pay (PRP) schemes are often encouraged. PRP can reflect an individual's, team's or company's performance. As mentioned earlier, it is difficult to calculate, particularly if it relates to individual performance, hence most schemes reflect company performance.

The advantages of company performance schemes are that they are easy to calculate; they do not pay out if the company cannot afford it and employees in support areas (catering, administration, etc.) also receive a benefit. The disadvantages are that they do not reflect an individual's performance (good or bad) and factors outside of the employees control may limit the pay out, e.g. exchange rates, share dividends, recession.

Team PRP encourages team members to support lower performers and individuals can see the results of their efforts far more than with company performance schemes. On the down side, consistently slow individuals may be bullied or 'encouraged' to leave. Stress levels of struggling team members may be high and inter-team rivalry and friction may develop, particularly if one team can affect the performance of another.

With individual PRP, it is easy to see the link between individual effort and reward, which motivates individuals to achieve objectives. It does, however, run the risk of dispiriting the individual if the scheme is poorly designed and it does not encourage teamwork.

Kohn (1993) challenges the effectiveness of any form of PRP as follows:

- Pay is a dubious motivator (p. 38).
- Financial rewards are a short-term motivator.
- Financial rewards alter behaviour but not the underlying attitudes or commitment.
- The more cognitively difficult a job is, the more tenuous the link with PRP.
- PRP discourages risk taking.

Kohn suggests that companies should concentrate on the intrinsic motivational factors such as the job itself (see p. 38).

Job satisfaction

Closely linked with motivation is the idea of job satisfaction:

'a pleasant or positive emotional state resulting from the appraisal of one's job' (Locke, 1976).

If individual employees are motivated in their job they are likely to be satisfied. Unfortunately, there is plenty of evidence that many are dissatisfied at work (see RLA 4). Consequently, organizations are increasingly using satisfaction surveys. In these surveys, employees complete a series of questions concerning both intrinsic and extrinsic motivators, along with the way they are treated, their trust in their manager and the company's communications. The results are trended (compared to previous years) to see if any factor is getting worse and action

plans are put in place to try to resolve any issues.

There is criticism of such surveys, particularly as they generally involve employees using a rating scale to indicate their answers. The general nature of the questions makes an accurate rating difficult and the mood of the employees or lack of interest in the survey may lead to inaccurate responses. Focus groups and interviews with people who are leaving the company often produce more useful data about the satisfaction levels and issues of the workforce.

Real Life Application 4:

Britons are most dissatisfied workers in Europe

Only 36 per cent of Britons say they enjoy work (see Table 2.3). Longer hours, the nightmare of commuting and worries about job security make the British among the most miserable workers in Europe, according to a survey by Oswold and Blanchflower (2000). They based their findings on interviews held with 19 000 workers from 25 countries.

Table 2.3: Percentage of employees who are 'very satisfied' with their job (Oswold and Blanchflower, 2000)

Rank	Country	Percentage
1	Denmark	62
2	Philippines	61
3	Cyprus	60
4	Switzerland	53
5	Israel*	52
6	Spain	50
7	Netherlands	49
	US	49
9	Israel**	47
10	New Zealand	41
11	Sweden	40
12	Canada	39
	Portugal	39
	Russia	39
	Germany (west)	39
16	Norway	37
17	Britain	36
18	Italy	35
19	Bangladesh	33
20	France	32
21	Germany (east)	31
22	Japan	30
23	Czech Republic	28

24	Poland	27
	Slovenia	27
26	Bulgaria	26
27	Hungary	23

*Arab workers only
**Jewish workers only

Professor Oswold commented on Britain's low ranking:

'Britain's result is worrying because the bulk of the countries below us are Eastern Europeans and have poor working conditions.'

Asked why Britons are so miserable, he explained:

'Firstly, job security has got worse in Britain relative to other countries. Secondly, we are working longer hours now, a number of hours more than our competitors in Europe. Commuting times have risen, particularly in the South East, as a result workers are away from their families for longer periods. This is affecting not just their job satisfaction but mental well-being.'

The survey tends to confirm a general trend over the past 25 years. In the 1973 General Household Survey, 42.7 per cent of Britons said they were happy with their jobs, ten years later that number had fallen to 39 per cent. Similar studies in the 1990s confirm the downward trend. Since 1991 though, workers in Holland, Germany and Spain have all climbed above Britain, believing themselves to be happier at work.

Article adapted from 'Job dissatisfaction',
Daily Mail, 10 May 2000.

Summary

- Job satisfaction in Britain appears to have been declining for 25 years.
- Current explanations include lack of job security, longer working hours and longer commuting.

Questions

1 Why do you think other countries appear to have more satisfied workers?

2 In order to assess the reliability of the survey data in Table 2.3, what other information would it be important to know?

What causes satisfaction?

Hachman and Oldman (1975) grouped the main determinates of job satisfaction into five groups, very similar to those affecting motivation:

- **Skill variety** – the extent to which the job requires a range of skills.
- **Task identity** – the extent to which the worker can complete a whole job, not just a part of it.
- **Task significance** – its impact on others.
- **Autonomy** – the level of choice and discretion allowed.
- **Feedback** – how much performance and outcome feedback is given.

Job satisfaction and improved performance

It is easy to conclude that satisfied workers must perform better. However, Affalden and Muchussly (1985) found the correlation to be only 0.17, meaning that there is only a slightly greater chance of people being more productive if they are satisfied.

Smith and Brannick (1993) state that it is not participation that increases job satisfaction and performance, but the improvement of employees' expectations. They draw upon Schuler's work (1977) concerning participation in decision making; role conflict; role ambiguity; performance outcome, expectancy and job satisfaction. Schuler's conclusion was that *participation in decision making is effective in increasing job satisfaction* not because of the participation but its effects on expectancy and role stress.

Stress

One major demotivator and cause of job dissatisfaction is stress. Since the early 1990s greater emphasis has been placed by organizations on monitoring and reducing the stress levels of employees, the main reason not being altruism but the increasing number of successful legal claims against employers. While stress is rarely totally due to work, it can have a devastating effect on individuals.

Stress process

The stress process starts with a trigger or stressor. These can be individual, such as bereavement or cumulative typified by comments like 'I have had a bad week'. Generally, people can cope if they have the support of others and engage in coping behaviours, the simplest of which is to take deep breaths before facing the stressor again. The reactions to stress vary from person to person, however in different degrees there are physiological, emotional and behavioural reactions (see Table 2.4).

Physiological reactions

Walter Cannon in 1929 discovered that the stress response is part of a unified (all one) mind-body system. He tested individuals by exposing them to extremes of temperature and emotional events and saw an increase in adrenaline and noradrenaline. These are stress hormones produced by the adrenal glands in response to two processes which will occur in parallel and are referred to as the dual response system (see Figure 2.12).

In addition to the release of cortisol triggered by the sympathetic nervous system, there are other physiological effects:

- increased heart rate
- increased breath rate
- blood diverted to skeletal muscles
- fat released ready for energy conversion.

Cannon called this response the **fight or flight** response typified by the image of early humans making life or death decisions around whether to fight the oncoming animal or run. In modern day, crossing a busy road, confronting an angry customer or getting on a crowded train triggers the same response.

Following on from Cannon's work, researchers have found that the outer part of the adrenal gland also releases the stress hormone cortisol, on instructions from the cerebral cortex (see Figure 2.12).

Selye (1976) while researching sex hormones found more responses to stress and saw that the responses varied depending upon the type of stress. Selye called this three-stage process, the **General Adaption Syndrome (GAS)**. **Stage 1** is the **alarm reaction** caused by the sympathetic nervous system (see above). Once the reaction is complete the person is ready to face the challenge (**stage 2 resistance**). During this period body temperature, blood pressure and respiration remain high. If this persists then the stress may deplete the body's reserves (**stage 3 exhaustion**) With exhaustion people are more vulnerable to illness or even death. It is this factor in particular that worries medical authorities and employers.

Stress and heart disease

One of the most frightening physiological reactions to stress is the impact it has on coronary heart dis-

Table 2.4: How people cope with and react to stress

Stressors	Coping factors	Stress reactions
Disasters	Family support	Physiological
Work pressures	Re-evaluation of the situation	Emotional
Relationship problems	Pleasant distractions	Behavioural
Money worries	Coping behaviours	

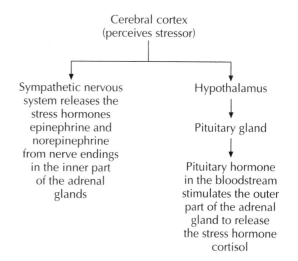

Figure 2.12: Dual response system

ease, the western world's leading cause of death. Highly elevated levels of cortisol have in particular been found to lower the immune system and thereby potentially lead to illness. While there are many factors that increase the risk of heart disease, Friedman and Roseman (1956) discovered that stress is a factor (see Key Study 4).

A further study of 3000 healthy men identified that very broadly, people fall into two categories:

- **Type A** – competitive, impatient, verbally aggressive, hyper aware of time.
- **Type B** – basically far more easy going in all of these factors.

Over a nine-year study, 257 of the men suffered a heart attack, 69 per cent of whom were Type A. Not only were Type A people twice as likely to have a heart attack but not one person regarded as being 'very easy going' had suffered one.

Commentary

Remember the risks of stress as you revise for your exams or rush around at work! While a fundamental 'calming down' would appear to be required to avoid a heart attack, regular exercise, relaxation techniques, a good diet, not smoking and annual full medicals can also reduce risks. In addition, if you find your job forces

---

KEY STUDY 4

Researchers: Friedman and Roseman (1956, 1984)

Aims: To identify any physiological changes brought on by work pressures.

Method: They tested the blood cholesterol levels and blood clotting speed of 40 tax accountants regularly throughout a one-year period.

Results: From January to March, the levels remained stable. As the April tax return deadline approached the accountants' cholesterol and clotting rates rose to dangerous levels. By mid-May the levels had returned to normal.

Conclusions: That work pressures have an adverse physiological impact on the human body.

---

you to be Type A, then maybe a change of career is called for!

Stress also reduces the immune system's effectiveness. Jemmoch and Locke (1984) exposed animals to stress and identified a significant increase in susceptibility to disease. Cohen *et al* (1992) compared a group of monkeys exposed to stress against a calmer control group. Once again the stressed animals showed lower immune defences.

Stress is also linked to cancer as tumours develop faster when the immune system is depressed.

Emotional and behavioural responses

While some physiological reactions might not be noticeable in someone who is stressed, emotional and behavioural symptoms are far more obvious, particularly if they are out of character.

Out-of-character stress reactions include:

- loss of short-term memory
- short temper
- undue upset over trivial matters
- missing deadlines
- increased work absence/lateness
- increased emotional state
- increased accident rate.

Commentary

While there can be many causes for these symptoms,

managers should look out for them and discuss the symptoms with any employee who is displaying them (particularly if the employee is also displaying physical symptoms such as headaches, painful stomach, e.g. irritable bowel syndrome, and poor skin condition).

Causes of work stress

There are many causes of stress at work, which when coupled with stress from an employee's home life, can cause many of the symptoms discussed above. Many researchers have identified causes such as:

- too much or too little work
- personality
- too complex job
- work life conflicting with home life
- uncertainty about the role
- conflict
- too greater responsibility
- being responsible for others
- time pressures
- highly repetitive work
- working shifts
- salary levels lowering compared to others
- prospect of redundancy
- dangerous environment.

Women and stress

As women increasingly return to work full time and aim for careers, there is a likelihood that they will increasingly suffer from the stress-related illnesses more typically found in men. In a 20-year study into heart disease in Framington, USA (Cooper 1988), overall it was found that working women do not have a significantly higher incidence of coronary heart disease than housewives. Married working women, however, with families to look after as well as a job, did have an increased incidence. This rate rose as the number of children increased.

Newberry *et al* (1979) examined psychiatric status and social adjustment of a group of working married women and housewives from the same community. There were no discernible differences apart from working women being less interested in housework and housewives having a greater feeling of inadequacy.

Welner *et al* (1979) did, however, find that women GPs suffer from a significantly higher rate of psychiatric depression than a control group and that those with children were found to have more career disruption, a cause of stress.

Causes more common with women

While women are affected by the same causal factors as men, they have (in varying degrees) the additional pressures of:

- **sex stereotyping** (belief that women can only do certain jobs)
- **low expectation** (if females are told often enough that women don't go far, then expectations lower)
- feeling of **inadequacy**
- **less assertive** than males
- **avoiding success** to behave in a more socially accepted manner (Horner, 1970)
- **male bosses** often either protect the female staff, thereby not exposing them to the same developmental events as males or they may feel threatened by a young up and coming female.
- **sexual involvement** – inevitably many relationships form in the workplace, therefore females experience sexual pressure, and possibly harassment from males who may have an influence over their future
- **balancing home and work life**
- **blocked promotion** for many of the reasons listed above – often referred to as the 'glass ceiling', i.e. women can see the jobs but can't get there
- feelings of **guilt** as not at home when children need them.

Commentary

When you review the list of causes of stress in women, it is amazing that men still have a higher level of stress-related illnesses and shorter life spans. Evolutionists would put that down to the female body needing to be able to care for young children to ensure the survival of the species (whereas the man in theory only needs to be there at the conception!). Therefore it is natural that females should be more resistant to factors such as pain and stress.

Many organizations are trying to reduce stress in all employees but in particular are attempting to influence some of the factors specific to women (see RLA 5). Examples include: career breaks, so that women can return to work more easily once their children start school; flexible working hours; and working from home. Sexual harassment programmes are designed both to stop the harassment and educate people as to the options open to them if they are harassed. (Sexual harassment is primarily but not solely aimed at women.) The glass ceiling is increasingly being smashed although female managers still tend to earn less than their male colleagues.

Real Life Application 5: Work and family

With unemployment in the USA at a 25-year low, employers everywhere are looking for ways to rise above their competitors. Appearing in the *Working mothers magazine* annual 100 best companies list appears to be one method.

More recently, two other prestigious magazines, *Business week* and *Fortune*, have also run awards for family friendly companies.

First Tennessee Bank, which is ranked in all three lists, believes that profits start with satisfied employees and with that formula revenue has grown 4 per cent per year more than the industry average.

The awards look for opportunities for women to advance, child care benefits, flexible working, paternity leave plus ongoing efforts to improve, even if the company was ranked highly the year before. If a company is predominantly female but as a proportion, males are the highest earners, they stand no chance of being rated. In the *Business week* award, 4500 employees are asked questions such as 'Can you vary your work hours to respond to family matters?', 'Do you feel comfortable taking time off work to attend to family matters?'.

The front running companies tend to have visionary leaders with a culture of inspiring employees. Many offer onsite gyms, child care and dry cleaners. Those interviewed tended to describe working there as being fun. Consistently, those ranked high, showed financial results ahead of industry averages.

Article adapted from 'An inside look at making the grade' by Michelle Neely Martinez, *HR Magazine*, March 1998.

Reprinted with the permission of *HR Magazine*, published by the Society for Human Resource Management (www.shrm.org), Alexandria, VA, USA.

Summary

- Increasingly in the USA, family friendly companies are being recognized through national awards.
- Winning companies make work life flexible and offer onsite facilities. They appear to be reaping financial rewards as a result of this approach.

Working shifts

Another cause of stress is breaking the natural circadian rhythm that encourages humans to sleep at night. Working at night is not natural. A person's body temperature falls during the small hours of the morning and Kleinman (1963) monitored the reaction times of a group and showed a correlation with oral temperature – as body temperature fell naturally with the circadian rhythm, the group's reaction times reduced (see Figure 2.13).

While this study did not prove a causal link, Kleinman felt that it was a major factor. Further studies by Rutenfrang *et al* (1970) could not find a correlation between temperature and reaction time but did agree that reaction time varies by some unknown factor in the circadian rhythm.

The adverse effects of shift work are exaggerated further if the shift patterns vary (Sigman, 1993), for instance one month of days followed by a month of nights, or a rolling shift (week 1: 6 am–3 pm; week 2: 3 pm–11 pm; week 3: 11 pm–6 am).

There is also an increased incidence of accidents at night as reaction times lower. While obviously major accidents happen during the day as well, the explosions at the Chernobyl nuclear power plant in the Soviet Union in 1986 and at the Bhopal chemical plant in India in 1984, both classified as 'human error' accidents, happened at night.

Stressful occupations

Some occupations are by their very nature more stressful than others. If combined with a Type A personality, the possibility of a stress-related illness is increased. Well-documented stressful occupations include teaching, the emergency services and offshore drilling. The reasons for their association with stress are reasonably obvious. However, other stressful occupations include retailing, call centre operators and production line workers. With retailing and other customer service roles it is primarily the actions of the customers that cause the stress, while call centres are often accused of being high pressure environments where if calls are not answered at specific rates, job security is affected. Production line workers are often stressed due to the monotony and lack of control over their workload.

Unemployment and redundancy

With so much evidence pointing towards work causing stress, unemployment might logically be thought of as beneficial. However, to those who have experienced being unemployed or being made redundant, the stress of working seems minor. Warr

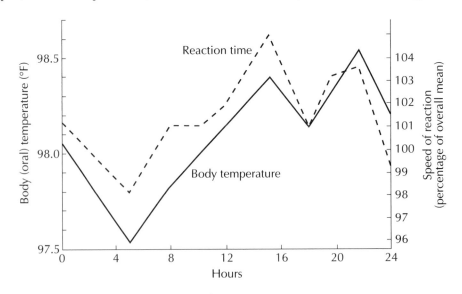

Figure 2.13: Body temperature and reaction time over 24 hours

From N. Kleitman, *Sleep and Wakefulness* (1963), University of Chicago Press

Unemployment causes stress

(1984) and other researchers have found that the trauma of being made redundant is similar to bereavement with the same stages of shock, shattered self-image and readjustments to be worked through. The resulting lower self-image and expectations can lead to lower motivation to retrain or make significant life changes to find work.

Fryer and Payne (1986) suggested that people who experience unemployment often suffer from lower levels of personal happiness, self-esteem and psychological well-being, along with increased depression, difficulty in concentrating and other behavioural problems.

Unemployment also affects the physical well-being of the individual, for instance increased levels of breathing and heart conditions.

Why is unemployment stressful?

Aside from the financial pressures, Jahoda (1979) found that employment provides:

- structuring of time
- social contact (other than family)
- personal status
- goals and objectives
- social credibility.

When someone becomes unemployed these factors are lost, leading to negative psychological states.

Retirement

The factors listed by Johoda also apply to retirement, so is retirement stressful? While a job is a socially defined and acceptable role, retirement has been described as the 'roleless role' and for some the lack of a role is distressing. Those who have prepared for retirement by part-time working, developing new social circles and hobbies, find the transition less stressful.

Commentary

The transition to retirement can be stressful, often belied by the fact that when recent retirees return to visit former colleagues, they always look so well! Many companies now provide retirement training to help with these pressures. Normally starting two years before retirement the courses for the employee and their partner cover financial planning; health and fitness; psychological changes, potential stressors and how to avoid them.

Those who retire early often find the experience leads to boredom, depression and loneliness (Cooper, 1979).

Psychological contract

A further cause of stress is the breaking of the psychological contract.

Schein (1978) states:

'Through various kinds of symbolic and actual events "a psychological contract" is formed which defines what the employee will give in the way of effort and contribution in exchange for challenging or rewarding work.'

Schein is describing what he refers to as 'a mutual acceptance' and indicates various events that signal 'you have been accepted' by your organization. These signals include:

- positive appraisal
- salary increase
- new job assignment
- sharing of secrets
- uniforms
- clubs
- initiation events.

Employees' acceptance of the organization is shown by:

- their decision to remain
- a high level of motivation and commitment
- willingness to accept various kinds of constraints, delays or undesirable work.

The subsequent psychological contract:

'changes in important ways as the person goes through a career and life cycle … similarly what the organization expects of the individual changes with changes in job or role' (Schein, 1978).

Watson (1994) reinforces this view that out of work factors are important when considering the psychological contract, i.e. lack of promotion prospects, new family, etc. Furthermore, Watson (1987) (who talks of an implicit rather than psychological contract) states that the contract is never fixed nor is it ever stable and two major factors tend to threaten stability:

- The push towards increased efficiency on the part of the employer.
- The tendency towards collective action and challenge on the part of the employee.

Robinson and Rousseau (1994) ascertain that violating the psychological contract is not the exception but the norm and therefore a common cause of dissatisfaction in the workforce.

Essay questions

1 Discuss the various psychological theories as to why people go to work. (23)

2a Herzberg used the phrase 'hygiene factors' to describe what most writers later called 'extrinsic motivators'. What are extrinsic motivators and why did Herzberg call them 'hygiene factors'? (10)

2b Taking a company or industry with which you are familiar, discuss how extrinsic and intrinsic motivators are used. (13)

3a What are some of the main causes of stress in the workplace? (10)

3b What is the physiological effect of stress?

3 Leadership

This chapter considers how managers or leaders motivate, direct and oversee those working for them. The process of communication is then discussed as this is one of the vital factors in ensuring employee effectiveness and satisfaction. Real Life Applications that are considered are:

- RLA6: No return to shirt and tie at BT
- RLA7: The John Lewis Partnership
- RLA8: NLP and military accounting
- RLA9: Why it's good to talk.

Manager or leader?

A **manager** is someone who formally holds authority over subordinate workers. A **leader,** however, could be anyone – a child in a playground game, a chief antagonist in a riot or the person who gets everyone back on track when disaster strikes. The words manager and leader are often used interchangeably.

A manager is an example of an **official leader**, whereas the others are **unofficial leaders**. Both may be displaying **leadership behaviours.** In many instances, unofficial leaders appear in the work environment, because they are either assertive, talented, experienced, very aggressive or in a position of power such as a union official. The unofficial leader can undermine the authority of the official leader or can be very useful to the official leader if he or she is supportive. Unofficial leaders who show a positive attitude tend subsequently to get promoted to management positions or take on more responsibility.

McKenna (1994) gives the following description of leadership and management:

'Leadership is a force that creates capacity among a group of people to do something that is different or better. This could be reflected in a more creative outcome, or a higher level of performance. In essence, leadership is an agency of change and could entail inspiring others to do more than they would otherwise have done or were doing. By contrast management is a force more preoccupied with planning, co-ordinating, supervising and controlling routine activity, which of course can be done in an inspired way. Managerial leadership could be viewed as an integral part of the managerial role and its significance grows in importance as we move up the organizational hierarchy.'

Leadership

Leadership comprises the competencies, personal qualities, behaviours and style of a leader. It is possible for someone to show leadership qualities and not be a manager, in fact at selection interviews, this is often what is being looked at.

Leadership has been researched actively, the following questions have been asked in particular:

- What characteristics do leaders have?
- Are there different styles of leadership and if so which is best?
- How do effective leaders differ from ineffective leaders?
- Are effective leaders born that way or can they be trained?

Characteristics of leaders

Many studies have been completed on the characteristics that leaders display. More recently, a whole raft of leadership competencies has been identified, such as the competency wheel shown in Figure 1.26 on p. 30, which is for managers within a global company. There is some doubt, however, as to the value of identifying such competencies. Work by Yetton (1984) concludes that there is little conclusive evidence for associating specific competencies with leadership, let alone effective leadership.

The debate has brought a certain level of consensus in that different situations will require different behaviours or competencies and that **behaviour** (the visible sign of **personality traits**) is an important influence on how effective a leader is.

Personality traits

A trait is an individual characteristic in thought,

feeling and action, either inherited or acquired, and refers to tendencies to act or react in certain ways.

Traits can be categorized in four ways:

- **Motive traits** – behaviour influenced by goals. Motivation surveys look at this trait.
- **Ability traits** – possessing specific skills influences natural behaviour.
- **Temperament traits** – e.g. depression, outgoing.
- **Stylistic traits** – the way individuals do something as opposed to what they do.

The traits that have been commonly identified in leaders include:

- intelligence
- self confidence
- dominance
- activity level
- technical and task knowledge
- self assurance
- need for achievement
- decisiveness.

Skills

In addition to personality traits, effective leaders tend to possess certain skills (which may be affected by traits), in particular:

- oral communication
- human relations skills
- resistance to stress
- assertiveness
- ability to construct and maintain social order
- knowledge of their environment
- ability to develop a network of colleagues
- time management.

Commentary

You will probably have already started to notice that some skills mentioned seem to be a trait and vice versa. This highlights why the word competency is now used as it combines skills, style traits and values.

Styles and approaches to leadership

Equipped with a combination of traits, skills and values, coupled with influences from past experiences and the culture of the working environment, leaders will tend to adopt certain styles. Kurt Lewin (1930, 1958) first started moving away from solely looking at traits towards behavioural styles (see Key Study 5).

Lewin saw leadership style as ranging from autocratic through to laissez-faire and this scale has

---

KEY STUDY 5

Researcher:	Kurt Lewin (1930s)
Aims:	To identify how group performance varies under different conditions, in particular under varying leadership styles.
Method:	Groups of children were given tasks such as model making and various styles of leadership ranging from autocratic (do it now) through to laissez-faire (no real control) were employed. The method by which the models were made, the way instruction and praise were given and the rules of the group reflected the different approaches.
Results:	The groups appeared to act more favourably to a more democratic approach where everyone was involved in decision making. There was less aggression and far more group unity than with groups who had autocratic managers.
Conclusions:	That autocratic leadership styles are less effective than more democratic approaches.
Critics:	In different cultural settings different results were gained (Lewin's work was done in Nazi Germany). Difficult to apply same results to adults working in industry.

---

influenced many subsequent studies. The typical scales used to show the possible range of styles tend to include those shown in Figure 3.1.

Task and person orientation

A further common finding was that leaders tended to have a tendency towards being very focused either on getting the task completed or on the needs of the team. This was initially identified by studies in the 1950s at Ohio State University. These studies identified ten main leadership behaviours but saw that they could be grouped in two ways (Fleishmann, 1962):

- **Consideration** – the extent to which a leader

Autocratic	Consultative/democratic	Participative	Laissez-faire
Instructs and motivates through fear	Involves team on major issues and bears views in mind. Open communication	Involves others in most decisions and allows them to make many own decisions	Complete free reign Anarchy

Figure 3.1: Leadership styles

demonstrates trust of subordinates, respect for their ideas and consideration of their feelings.

- **Structures** – the extent to which a leader defines and structures his or her own role and those of subordinates (those reporting to the leader) towards obtaining that goal. The leader actively directs group activities through planning, communicating information, scheduling, criticizing and trying out new ideas.

The studies concluded that effective managers tended to be the ones who seemed concerned about their subordinates whereas ineffective managers were only concerned with the task.

These two styles were later picked up by Blake and Mouton (1985) with the **Managerial Grid**, where they are shown as two continuums (see Figure 3.2). The individual can score anything between 9,9, i.e. very strong on both scales down to 1,1, i.e.

displays neither. The ideal is to move towards the 9,9 rating where there is a similar strong concern for the team and the task in hand.

Other styles include 9,1 (task management) where the manager focuses solely on getting the task done. If this style is used continually, staff are likely to be demotivated. This style is not uncommon in people with high levels of technical skill and drive, but low interpersonal skills. This style was common in many manufacturing environments where it was felt that shopfloor workers were predominately Theory X (see p. 42) and needed to be treated accordingly.

At the other extreme is the 1,9 or country club approach where the emphasis is on the people to the exclusion of getting the task done. Even if people make mistakes or miss deadlines, it is overlooked and conflict is actively avoided. This is sometimes seen in weak, unassertive managers in environments

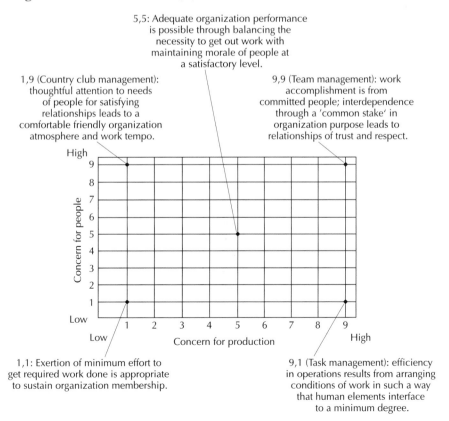

Figure 3.2: Blake and Mouton's (1985) Managerial Grid

where there is little competition and few financial pressures.

Participation

On Lewin's scale and towards 9,9 on the Managerial Grid is the notion of a participative style of leadership. This concerns the extent to which the leader shares information with subordinates, encouraging questions and helping them to communicate with each other.

Another commonly used scale shows the potential differences in this approach:

- **Tells** – the leader makes a decision and then announces it with no consultation.
- **Sells** – the leaders makes the decision, then tries to convince everyone that it is the correct one. This is often regarded as the weakest style of management.
- **Consults** – the leader asks subordinates their opinion before making a decision, although he may choose to ignore their views.
- **Delegates** – the leader allows the subordinates to make the decisions.

Commentary

Remember that leaders do not simply fit into the styles described by the headings. With this and Lewin's scale, a leader could be at any point on the scale, e.g. if rated between Tells and Sells he or she will display characteristics of both.

Tasks that have increasingly tended to be dealt with in a participative manner include:

- budgeting
- process design
- quality
- health and safety
- empowerment.

Budgeting

Employees are affected by budgets, i.e. how much money must come in (sales) and how much can be spent and on what. This is typically a very complex and no win situation, with subordinates often feeling that the sales targets are too high and the resources they can afford are insufficient. Increasingly, input to the budget process is being encouraged from all of those who will be impacted by it. This is partly so that they have a stake in the final budget and will tend to agree with it more and also so that more information, including that unknown to the accountants, is used to form an accurate budget.

Process design

Particularly in manufacturing where the principle of Kaizen (continuous improvement) is employed, shopfloor workers are being asked either to make suggestions or be actively involved in decisions relating to process design, the principle being that they are the experts and know what works and what doesn't. This approach is now employed in administrative environments too where, traditionally, specialized systems designers would organize the work flow. Mumford (1980) is an advocate of this approach believing that 'consensus participation' is an effective means of getting every user's input into new systems.

Quality

Quality circles are an example of a formal participative tool. Here employees come together to discuss quality issues relating to their area and provide solutions. For many, this may be the only meetings that their job involves, so training often has to be given if the process is to be effective.

Suggestion schemes are another method of inputting ideas for improvements. Sometimes a financial reward is given if the suggestion is taken up. The Japanese culture promotes suggestion schemes and in companies such as Toyota any suggestion that would improve a process by more than a few seconds or save more than £100 is carried out. In many Japanese companies a whole level of management is required in order to review all of the suggestions. One employee at Matsushita contributed 10 000 in one year.

Giving employees the skills and authority to check their own work and make corrective decisions is a good example of participative leadership.

Health and safety

In light of legal changes that make health and safety everyone's responsibility, all employees are being encouraged to monitor and correct any health and safety issue.

Empowerment

Empowerment was mentioned as one means of motivating employees and there is some evidence that shows empowered workers are more satisfied.

Empowerment is often used interchangeably with terms such as **employee involvement** or **participa-**

tion, however it is a totally different paradigm. Lashley and McGoldrick (1994) sum up the difference:

'Empowerment is individual and personal: it engages the employee at the level of emotion, it is about discretion, autonomy, power and control and it is about responsibility, commitment and enterprise, it is also about goals.'

This is a step further than either employee participation, where employees get involved with decision making, or employee involvement, where employees identify with the aims and needs of the organization. Empowerment then gives them the means to achieve these aims. Marchington (1995) also tackles the misuse of the term and confirms that in most instances the reality falls short of the word's true meaning:

'which is to give an employee the power, authority and influence to do things at work'.

Collins (1994) states that:

'What is termed empowerment only equates to involvement and job participation since workers lack any voice in formulation of policy matters or strategic concerns ... instead workers are now offered involvement in a narrow way'.

Empowerment is the culmination of all of the aspects of participative leadership. In practical terms it means that to varying degrees, employees are not just consulted but are given ownership of certain processes or projects, leaving the manager to guide, coach and assist them. This requires a fundamental shift away from any autocratic approach and involves a high level of trust and risk taking. Consequently, many managers find this style difficult, particularly if the organization does not generally support such risks.

A further problem is that empowered employees can take it too far. Tom Peters, who has written widely on empowerment, cites a doorman working for Marriott hotels in the USA, who on seeing that a guest had left his briefcase behind, followed him to the airport to return it. On finding that he had already flown, the doorman got on the next flight and returned the case in person!

Commentary

Employees need to know the boundaries of their empowerment but by doing so the paradox of 'management making the decision for you that you can make decisions' is reinforced. It can also lead to frustration if employees feel that they are being told on the one hand

that they are empowered but are actually kept on a tight leash. In addition, some employees can be trusted to make major decisions while others lack the qualities to be able to do so. Inevitably, some employees end up being more empowered than others or everyone is empowered to the same degree which may restrict some or unleash others who will fail. An empowerment matrix is sometimes used to help control this (see Figure 3.3).

Individuals each agree a matrix with their manager. The aim at subsequent reviews of performance is to move more of the permissible tasks to the right, but this will depend upon training, previous success and performance.

Task description	Cannot do	Can do but must ask first	Can do but must inform me after	Can do
Raising orders		✓		

Figure 3.3: Empowerment matrix

Such a matrix is formalizing key aspects of the psychological contract and allows all concerned to know exactly what can and cannot be done. Empowerment is, on the whole, a key motivator but some people only want to come and work and do not want to make any decisions. They may in fact be demotivated by empowerment.

Moving to matrix structures

To support an environment where decision making is not just in a manager's remit, organizations need to be flatter, i.e. have few levels of management. This has the disadvantage though of limiting the possibilities for promotion and may mean that there simply are not enough managers to head up each project. In turn, flatter structures lead to managers having more people reporting to them than they did before. This is their span of control. If those people require little supervision and are empowered then a wide span of control is practical. If, however, the opposite applies then a narrow span of control is preferable.

With empowerment comes responsibility for decisions and projects that would formally have lain with management. Multiple projects may mean that there are many non-managers who for a particular project are the leader. This is called a matrix structure (see Figure 3.4) and was first put forward by FW Taylor in the early 1900s. Taylor was an advocate of the Scientific school of management which encouraged breaking processes down into parts and using teams to complete them.

	Project 1	Project 2	Project 3
Fred	Leader	Team member	Team member
Mohammed	Team member	Leader	Team member
Gail	Team member	Team member	Leader

Figure 3.4: Matrix responsibilities

In the example in Figure 3.4, one minute Fred is the leader while project 1 is being discussed, then Gail is the leader when the conversation turns to project 3. Matrix structures allow multiple projects to come on stream and be led. However, these may lead to friction as inevitably team members are going to have a preference for ensuring that their own project is completed before concentrating on ones that they do not lead. With no formal power over their colleagues, disciplinary and counselling situations can sometimes be overlooked.

Contingency approach

The American psychologist FE Fieldler (1967) believes that, on the whole, a task-centred approach is probably best for very structured work, i.e. with clear rules and procedures, it is also effective when work is unstructured and relationships between the manager and his or her team are poor, i.e. when conditions are unfavourable to the manager, then it may be best to take a firm stance. Fieldler believes that generally a **people-centred approach** is best for unstructured work, however again it depends upon the situation.

Fieldler proposes four variables that apply to these situations:

- emphasis on people or task (style)
- task structure
- manager-subordinate relationship
- power of the manager.

These variables can be assessed in order to identify the most appropriate approach. The style is identified by the manager rating his or her **least preferred co-worker (LPC)** and his or her **most preferred co-worker (MPC)**. Where the ratings are similar, then the manager is described as being a **high LPC leader** and is likely to be closer to his or her workforce and would tend to be people-centred in approach.

Where there is a big difference in the LPC and MPC ratings the manager is described as a **low LPC leader** and is likely to be distant from his or her subordinates and tend to be autocratic, task-orientated and less concerned with the human resources aspects of the role.

The **task structure** is another variable. If the organization provides rules, procedures, standards and measures for most tasks, then the leader and the subordinates have little room for discretion. It is easier to force compliance in a structured environment because of the lack of alternative approaches open to the subordinates. In an unstructured environment, the leader may have to pay more attention to coaching, motivating and inspiring his or her team.

The power held by a leader will partly reflect his or her skill and reputation but organizations also provide power to certain roles. Regardless of whether people disagree with a decision, they know that this leader must be obeyed.

Commentary

A task-orientated, high power approach has long been used in the military. Boot camp or basic training was designed to destroy any level of individual thought and encourage blind obedience, the principle being that in battle there is no time for a debate. This principle works fine if the leaders make the right decisions. However, in World War I when officer selection was based on family background, many leaders were very poor. As a result, many senseless advances (called 'going over the top') were made in order to gain just a few feet of land. In light of this, in World War II greater emphasis was placed on selecting officers with leadership traits. In modern times, rigorous training and selection are used to ensure that ineffective leaders are identified early.

'Going over the top' – an example of poor leadership

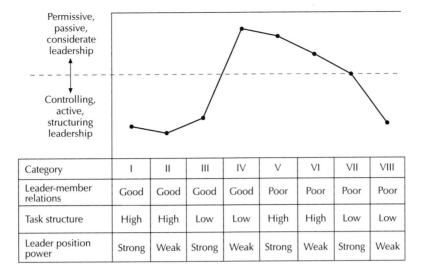

Category	I	II	III	IV	V	VI	VII	VIII
Leader-member relations	Good	Good	Good	Good	Poor	Poor	Poor	Poor
Task structure	High	High	Low	Low	High	High	Low	Low
Leader position power	Strong	Weak	Strong	Weak	Strong	Weak	Strong	Weak

Figure 3.5: Contingency model of leadership effectiveness

FE Fiedler 'Median Correlations between leader LPC scores and group performance measures obtained in original and validation studies (only)'. Vol. 17, No. 4, Fig. 1. Reprinted from 'The effects of leadership training and experience: a contingency model interpretation' by FE Fiedler, published by *Administrative Science Quarterly*, December, 455. By permission of *Administrative Science Quarterly*.

The relationship between the leader and his or her team is also important. A leader who is liked and respected is likely to be able to make hard decisions that a lesser thought of leader would not get away with. Similarly, a team may complete difficult tasks when the leader plays on his or her relationship with the team to motivate.

Fieldler produced a continuum that shows which style is likely to be effective in different situations (see Figure 3.5). In category I a controlling style would be effective as the task structure is high, the power of the leader is also high and the relations between leader and team are good. In category IV, a more people-orientated approach is preferred as relationships are good, there is low task structure and the leader's role wields little official power.

John Adair (1990) has built upon other contingency approaches and proposes that to be effective a leader must balance three sets of needs at the same time depending upon the situation (see Figure 3.6). Task needs are those that relate to the planning, goal setting and monitoring required to complete a task. The group needs are such aspects as: maintaining team spirit, ensuring team cohesion and discipline. The individual will also have specific needs and motivations and these should be addressed.

While the circles are the same size that does not mean that the three factors always have equal importance. The situation may require a greater emphasis on one, however overall over time, a balance should be visible.

Commentary

Contingency or situational approaches are best explained with an example. In most instances, a balance between the individual's needs, personality and experience must be made with the needs of the team and the task at hand. If, however, a rush order arrives that must be got out in half the usual time, the leader may have to make instant decisions and simply tell everyone what they must do and come down hard on anyone who is not working fast enough. Equally, in the case of a fire, a consultative approach, where everyone is spoken to politely and with respect, may not have the desired result!

Other approaches

There are many modern approaches to leadership that build on the models mentioned so far. In addition, certain techniques, processes and styles are influencing the way people are employed. In partic-

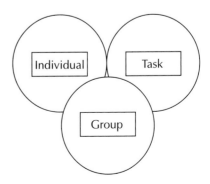

Fig 3.6: Situational leadership model, based on Adair (1990)

ular, new ways to motivate employees are being sought.

Transformational leadership

This is encouraged in unstable environments where, for instance, the life of a product may be very short or there is intense competition. Great emphasis is placed on recruiting and developing people who are creative and innovative. Leaders must also display these traits and be prepared to take risks, put the organization first and if necessary be directive. Other characteristics include:

- **charisma** – where a leader uses the power of his or her personality to elicit an effect on others
- **intellectual stimulation** – the leader is able to show subordinates new and creative ways of approaching old situations
- **emotional consideration** – displaying a high level of emotional intelligence (EI) (see p. 20)
- **vision** – having a view of where the organization is going and sharing that with all concerned.

Changes in work patterns and environments

Recently, a number of changes to work patterns and conditions have become more common. These include:

- **home working**
- **hot desking** – where employees do not have their own desk but just use any desk that is free
- **job sharing** – where a job is split into two part-time roles, but both employees hold the position and are responsible for the outcomes.

Flexible benefit packages

Companies such as BMW offer a flexible or 'cafeteria' approach to perks and benefits. As individual employees progress through the organization they are awarded points that can be used to 'buy' certain benefits, such as a better car, health insurance, pension contribution, holiday entitlement or cash. This allows individuals to bias their benefits towards their own **motivational needs**.

Dress down Friday

While some organizations have taken a more relaxed approach to dress generally (e.g. Microsoft), others have limited this to Fridays. On a Friday, employees can come dressed as they like (normally within reason), *the principle being that it is somehow motivational*. If, however, this was the case, then why not do it

everyday? The trend though is now reversing as there is evidence that the more casual dress code produces a more casual approach to work and encourages sexual harassment (see RLA 6).

Real Life Application 6:
No return to shirt and tie at BT

Hundreds of American corporations have reversed the decade-old trend of allowing casual clothes to be worn on Fridays.

A poll by the Society for Human Resource Management claims that the number of firms that allowed casual dress once per week has dropped from 97 per cent to 87 per cent over the last year. Another survey of 1000 companies claimed that more than 50 per cent of employees noticed an increase in the lateness and absenteeism of colleagues when dressed causally. More than 30 per cent also said that there was a rise in flirtatious behaviour and sexual jokes. There also appeared to be a general relaxation of work standards when not dressed smartly. Increasingly, workers, particularly in the dot.com companies, are returning to wearing suits, which is ironic as the casual approach started in silicon valley.

In the UK, BT and the accountancy firm Arthur Andersen stood by their decision to allow casual dress every day. Both companies stated that they felt people were more creative if dressed comfortably and had not noticed any change in behaviour or loss of productivity.

Article adapted from 'No return no shirt and tie at BT' by George Gordon, *Daily Mail*, 29 June 2000.

Summary

- Various surveys in the USA appear to indicate that fewer organizations are allowing casual dress at work.
- Anecdotal evidence indicates that there may be more flirting and a more casual attitude when employees are casually dressed.
- Two major UK employers continue to allow casual dress every day.

Questions

1 Comment on the reliability of the US surveys.

Communication

One of the key skills of a manager is communication (see competency wheel, Figure 1.26, p. 30) and satisfaction surveys consistently show that employees rate poor communication as a main cause of dissatisfaction. Every employee seems to have examples of where his or her company has communicated something badly. Most common are announcements about individual promotions or company site moves that leak out before those who are affected have been told. Every day examples tend to revolve around work that was found to be unnecessary if only the manager or another department had shared certain information.

Communication process

Communication can be shown as a cycle with five stages (all of which can easily go wrong) plus a constant threat of external influence, called noise, that could affect the message (see Figure 3.7).

Firstly, a message is encoded, i.e. the appropriate means of sending it is decided. Then the message is 'worded' as best as possible by the sender, then it is sent. At any point 'noise' can stop or alter the message. This could be:

- physical noise
- a poor translation
- a lack of attention by the receiver
- a technical fault with a phone or e-mail
- information overload where not all information can be taken in
- selectivity – some information is ignored
- rumours filling in the gaps that the official message left.

The message is then hopefully received. However, it may well be interpreted by the receiver as a different message to the one that was sent. This may be because of poor wording or because of the different perceptions or moods of the two parties.

The potential for communication problems is greater when there are multiple levels of communication, for instance a company chief executive tells senior managers one message and then they pass it

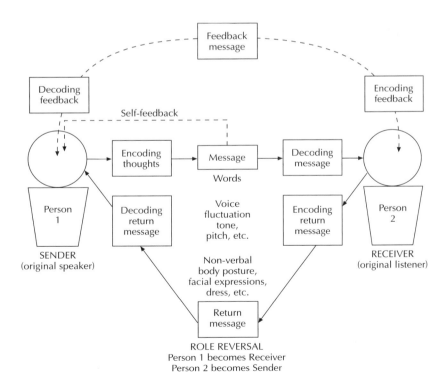

Figure 3.7: The communication cycle, based on Curtis and Detert (1981)

From *How to Relax: A Holistic Approach to Stress Management* by J D Curtis and R D Detert. Copyright © 1981 Mayfield Publishing Company. Reprinted by permission of the publisher.

on to the next level. It is not surprising that many employees receive a distorted message, if one at all.

Types of communication

Organizations must communicate effectively if they are to be efficient. Typical communications include: sales data from field sales staff to the head office; order details from the sales department to the production manager; information about new products or services, changes in staffing or proposed changes in working conditions. Information such as this would tend to be communicated through **official** or **formal** channels, e.g. team briefings, memos, intranet, e-mails, corporate videos, notices or meetings. They would probably not be communicated through **unofficial** or **informal** methods such as grapevine gossip, impromptu corridor chats or overheard conversations. In real life the grapevine often disseminates information very quickly, thereby causing distortion and possibly upsetting those who should have heard through official channels.

According to Davis (1976), a number of factors influence the creation of a grapevine:

- There is a lack of formal information.
- Some threat or insecurity sets rumours flying.
- Conflicts cause people to talk off the record.
- Distrust may cause disinformation to be circulated, possibly to stir up resistance or force a decision.
- Where there is a need to spread the information quickly, all too often decisions made in secret meetings are known to the staff by the time the manager gets back to his or her desk.

While managers generally find grapevines very frustrating, as they may adversely affect a carefully planned formal communication, some believe that their overall effect is positive. It is not unknown for managers to use the grapevine to spread information that they would prefer not to state formally. The researcher Zaremba (1988), who feels that grapevines offer an emotional safety valve and help to provide a feeling of belonging and security, shares this positive view. In addition, grapevines keep management on its toes and can help managers find out what is really going on in the organization.

The type and manner of communication may be influenced by its direction, for instance:

- **downwards** – generally formal messages from management to subordinates
- **upwards** – generally informal or passed via a representative such as a union official to the management
- **sideways** – both methods are used when communicating to a similar level within an organization.

It has long been thought that vertical (up and down) communication is the most effective. However, this has come into question following laboratory studies by Leavitt (1951) and Shaw (1964). Their research aimed to explore the effect of imposed communication networks on such things as problem solving and satisfaction. The test groups were only allowed to communicate with each other in writing according to the particular network being imposed.

Leavitt and Shaw used various networks where members could only communicate with certain other group members and the networks varied in their level of centralization i.e. having to go via one person to get to another (see Figure 3.8). The findings consistently showed that with simple problems, centralized networks are more effective whereas decentralized networks favour complex problems. A leader was also more likely to emerge in a centralized network. Satisfaction levels were highest in networks that offered the greatest combination of interactions and within that, the more central someone was, the greater his or her satisfaction.

Shaw (1964) puts the findings down to two factors:

- **independence** caused by a greater level of access to information, which in turn provides satisfaction
- **saturation** where centralized points in a network become overloaded or saturated with information during complex communications such as problem solving. This saturation leads to inefficiency.

Commentary

While such studies have been accused of being rather artificial they do indicate how the communication cycle can be aided or caused to fail in certain situations. They also provide an insight into the most effective way of laying out an office. For instance, people who sit opposite each other tend to communicate more. It makes sense therefore that people sit close to those that they need to communicate with the most.

Information passing up, down or around an organization will have to pass via various people, machines or systems. The structure and size of these networks has an immense influence on the speed

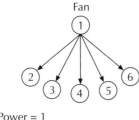

Fan

Power = 1

Communication restrictions = high

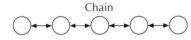

Chain

Power = 3

Communication restrictions = high

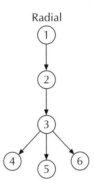

Radial

Power = 1

Communication restrictions = high

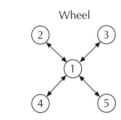

Wheel

Power = 1

Communication restrictions = high

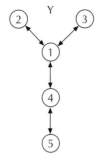

Y

Power = 1

Communication restrictions = high

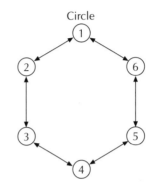

Circle

Power = equal

Communication restrictions = intermediate

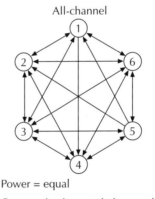

All-channel

Power = equal

Communication restrictions = nil

Figure 3.8: Examples of formal communication networks showing where the power lies

Betts

and effectiveness. With the rise of information and communications technology far more information is passing digitally, yet in many instances it still requires a human to read, interpret and respond to it. Pace (1983) identified some of the key roles and functions within a communication network:

- The **gatekeeper** – someone who occupies a position whereby he or she is able to control information either being sent or received. Such individuals can be at any point in the network.

- **Liaison** – someone who acts as a bridge between groups promoting closer relationships and ensuring that vital information is passed between them.
- **Cosmopolite** – someone who acts as a link between the organization and the outside world. He or she will have many contacts and provide valuable information on outside developments.
- **Isolate** – someone who tends to work alone and communicates little with others even if they hold vital information.

- **Isolated dyad** – two people who interact with each other a lot but communicate very little with others.

RLA 7 looks at one company's use of communication methods to keep its staff informed.

Real Life Application 7:

The John Lewis Partnership

With 41 000 employees working in its stores, the John Lewis Partnership faces the same problems as most large organizations concerning how to communicate information to its employees or partners as they are called.

The John Lewis Partnership is owned by its employees and as such has a culture of wanting to share as much business information as possible and encourage vertical communication. This is achieved through a variety of formal processes.

Each week two in-house magazines are produced and are sold to employees. *The Chronicle* is produced at the branch and contains sales information, features on changes within the store, minutes of meetings and official notices, along with more light-hearted articles about partners. *The Gazette* is produced centrally and includes sales information for each store, articles on new products or ventures, along with stories that wouldn't go amiss in a Sunday supplement. Both magazines are read intensely by most partners the day they come out.

One of the most daring features is that both magazines have letter pages in which any letter will be published, even if it is unsigned (only rude or legally sensitive letters are excluded). Any question other than salary information will be answered in that or a later issue.

Various committees allow shopfloor partners to communicate directly with senior managers. Branch councils cover issues relating to that branch. Central Council covers issues affecting the organization (similar to local and central government). The Committee for Communication covers day-to-day issues that may be only affect small groups or require a quick response, and Committee for Claims covers issues that affect individuals.

All other information is passed on at weekly departmental meetings called communication half hours.

Summary

- The John Lewis Partnership is owned by its employees and places a great emphasis on formal communication methods.

Questions

1 Why do you feel that formal communication methods are used so extensively in the John Lewis Partnership.

2 What other methods could they use?

3 What benefits could their effective communication network have for the organization?

Transactional analysis

Information flows between people (or machines) and is encoded and decoded. The role someone plays in that process affects the flow and nature of the information. This influence is affected by the personality, mood and perception of the individual.

Berne (1964) and Harris (1969) produced a very popular theory of personality and how it influences communication. They called this theory **Transactional Analysis (TA)** and it revolves around personality having three states, the Parent, Adult and Child. These states are not constant and the effectiveness of communication between people in the various states varies, therefore an understanding of TA allows someone to alter the message to communicate more effectively.

The **Parent** state is when people are particularly judgmental and moralistic. Often they are dogmatic, and self-righteous. They can, however, also be very protective of others, which is called being a nurturing parent. Visible cues to the parent state would be referring to rules and past experiences, shaking their head or a finger to express displeasure. Basically, they act as parents do with their children!

The **Adult** state is when individuals are the seeker or processor of information. They tend to be rational and objective. Preferably, TA should be used to ensure that at least one person takes up this role and leads the others.

The **Child** state is characterized by, as its name suggests, a child-like state, i.e. dependence, anxiety, immaturity, fear and hate. This would be noticeable by the individual's illogical responses, temper tantrums or attention-seeking behaviour.

With those states in mind, it is possible to use this information to improve communication. **Complementary transactions** are required to aid the process whereas **crossed transactions** are likely to fail. Complementary transactions consist of giving the other person the positive strokes, e.g. praise and recognition, that they deserve. If someone is clearly in a Child state then acting in the same way may allow a better understanding as long as one moves towards a Parent state. What the individual needs is a **nurturing parent** to sympathize and then slowly point out the lack of logic in the person's argument, finally to suggest a way forward that reduces the negative feelings of the Child.

The worst combinations are those that are crossed, for instance where the manager is acting like a parent and treating the subordinate as though he or she is in a Child state, and the subordinate does the same back. Such transactions are likely to lead to patronizing, and hostile conversations. The various combinations of transactions are shown in Figure 3.9.

Improving communication

There are many methods of improving communication:

- Select the most appropriate method.
- Select the most appropriate network.

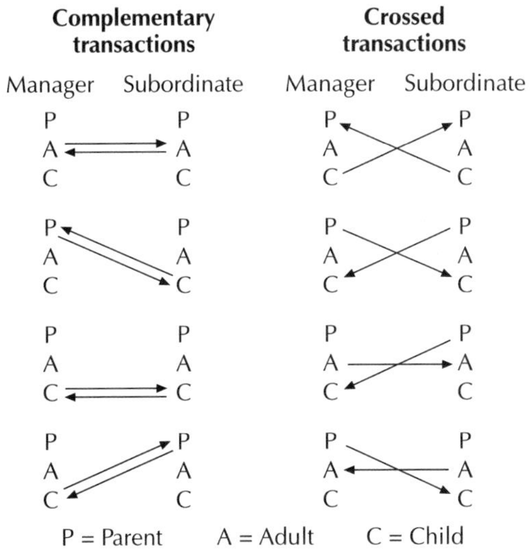

Figure 3.9: Examples of complementary and crossed communications

From *Effective business psychology* by DuBrin, © 1990. Reprinted by permission of Prentice-Hall, Inc., Upper Saddle River, N.J.

- Minimize noise.
- Train people to communicate clearly to avoid misinterpretation.
- Avoid information overload.
- Avoid calling meetings just to update everyone. If these are needed then it indicates that information flows are ineffective.
- Encourage two-way communication.
- Be aware of the various states and how to adapt to them (TA).
- Bear in mind the **perception** of the other person.

Perception

In the field of communication it is vital to understand that other people may see things differently, for instance an idea that appears to be excellent to one person may seem far too adventurous and risky to another.

Numerous techniques for doing this have become popular in the field of management. The two most commercially successful techniques (because you have to be trained in how to use them) are 'the seven habits of successful people' (Covey, 1989) and neuro linguistic programming.

Neuro linguistic programming

Once again debate rages about who developed the term neuro linguistic programming (NLP) and an industry has developed around it, with famous TV hypnotist Paul McKenna running regular NLP training courses.

NLP is a wide-ranging discipline that revolves around the words individuals use and how they affect the actions of that individual and others. For instance, an NLP practitioner would encourage people to say 'I will get that done by Friday' rather than 'I will do my best'. Certain words that are negative or defeatist should be excluded from your vocabulary as they immediately set your own motivation levels and those of others at second best.

NLP is very much concerned with changing the way people think to make them more positive and in control of their own destiny while displaying more enthusiasm. There are many aspects to NLP; three are described below.

Perceptual position

In NLP, users must acknowledge that there is a **first position** where someone looks at the world from his or her own point of view. A statement such as 'The way I see it is …' is an example of a first position.

A **second position** is looking at the world from another person's viewpoint and the **third position** is seeing both the former points of view and the relationship between the two. This is the way skilled negotiators work. They start by expressing the first position, then they go to the second position to see how it looks from everyone else's viewpoint, then they detach themselves and look at all of the views objectively. NLP practitioners compare this to the way the left eye sees one viewpoint, the right another but with both eyes, the brain produces a more rounded picture (see Figure 3.10)

Five logical levels

NLP, as mentioned, is concerned with analysing the words people use. In many discussions it is possible to use this interpretation to 'see where they are coming from'. In NLP speak it would be identifying their **logical level**.

The **first level (environment)** is where people are really talking about the place that they are and how they identify with it. For example, I can't do that *here* (as opposed to not being able to do it at all).

The **second level (behaviour)** is where people are concerned with what they actually do.

For example, I can't do *that* here (i.e. it's the particular action they have a problem with).

The **third level** is **capability**, whether people feel they have the ability to do something.

For example, I can't *do* that here (i.e. it's their capability to do it that's in question).

The **fourth level** is **beliefs and values** and it concerns what people believe to be true and important.

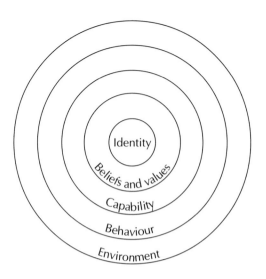

Figure 3.11: Five logical levels

McDermott and O'Connor

Individuals may not share the same values and beliefs as their manager or organization.

For example, I *can't* do that here (i.e. don't feel I should).

The **fifth level** is **identity**, people's sense of who they are and what they stand for.

For example, *I* can't do that here (i.e. you can, but I can't, it's just not me).

By identifying through questioning, observing body language and inflection within the statements, it is possible to see what level the person is communicating at and this enables a more effective response (see Figure 3.11).

Common language

NLP techniques centre around the words people use and where possible mirroring (copying) those words. People tend to perceive situations from different viewpoints and use language that reflects their perception. For instance, according to McDermott and O'Connor (1996) they may be:

- **visual words and phrases**
  - Look
  - Reflect
  - Clarify
  - The future looks bright
  - I see what you mean
  - Let's look closely at it
- **auditory**
  - Say, sound, tell, discuss
  - Turn a deaf ear
  - That message comes over loud and clear
  - In a manner of speaking

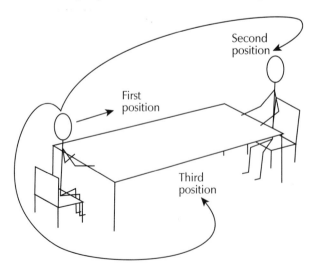

Figure 3.10: Three perceptual positions

McDermott and O'Connor

- **kinesthetic (actions)**
  - Touch, rough, grasp, hold
  - I will be in touch with you
  - Hold on
  - Too hot to handle.

Once the person's preferred way of communicating is identified, then an NLP practitioner can adapt his or her words to better 'turn on' the person they are dealing with. For example, the phrase 'I don't agree' is a neutral phrase – it doesn't contain verbal, auditory or kinesthetic words. To put this across in a more effective way to someone who has a preference for one of these styles, it could be said as:

- 'We don't see eye to eye' (visual)
- 'We are not on the same wave length' (auditory)
- 'Our ideas clash' (kinesthetic).

By matching language in this way or by using, for example, sporting or military metaphors (if the other person does) then he or she is likely to respond more positively (see RLA 8).

Real Life Application 8:
NLP and military accounting

In a large organization a consultant was called in to analyse why the accounts department was unable to communicate effectively with the rest of the organization. It was found that the rest of the company followed the lead of the senior management who used military metaphors to describe the business. Senior managers spoke of killing the competition, waging war on the market and shooting from the hip. The accounts department, however, did not possess any military experience, so instead used words such as credits, debits and budgets. The consultant translated all of these words into military speak or analogies (How much did you take from them? How much do you need to beat the others?) and the effect was very positive.

Article adapted from *Practical NLP for managers* by Ian McDermott and Joseph O'Connor, 1996.

Summary

- In this example, altering the metaphors used to better reflect those used by others improved communication.

Information technology

The rise of information technology (IT) in the workplace has drastically affected the way information is communicated. More information can be gathered, analysed, distributed and retrieved, far quicker than before. Bill Gates, the co-founder of Microsoft, calls this digital communication and refers to digital networks. In his book, *Business at the speed of thought*, Gates (1999) cites many examples of how organizations are utilizing digital technology to share, analyse and utilize information. One of the most common techniques is e-mail. The growth of e-mail has though caused a dramatic effect on interpersonal communication. It is far easier to communicate by e-mail than in person, particularly if the message needs to be spread to a wide audience. This ability unfortunately means that the numbers of e-mails that people receive compared to how many they require is out of proportion. This leads to information overload.

Other negative effects include:

- misinterpretation – humour, body language, tone of voice, all get lost when e-mail is used
- disturbance – new e-mails arriving disturb the work of those receiving them
- the destruction of communication networks – why bother going via someone, when you can e-mail them direct?
- subversive e-mails – by copying the note to important people it raises the profile of issues that wouldn't ordinarily be known at that level
- loss of people's ability to effectively communicate verbally, as their first response is to send an e-mail, even if it is to the person sitting next to them
- a decrease in the frequency of informal chats, thereby reducing the social element of job satisfaction (see RLA 9)
- harassment – it is easy to harass someone by e-mail as messages can go silently straight to them.

By being able to communicate so effectively by e-mail, many roles need not be based in an office and a new breed of 'e-lancers' has developed. E-lancers are people who work primarily via their computers, so location and meeting others is less important. To be an effective e-lancer requires excellent e-mail communication.

Ten rules for effective e-mailing (Wilkinson, 1999)

1 Remember that the recipient is human, include the niceties that would be used in person.
2 Be very polite and avoid typing LIKE THIS AS IT MEANS YOU ARE SHOUTING.
3 Image counts. Look good online, possibly by personalizing the look of your e-mails.
4 Respect privacy. Assume that you are the only one supposed to see that e-mail.
5 Share knowledge. Make sure everyone in the team knows what you know (as long as it is useful).
6 Keep focused. When people are busy, don't bother them with trivia.
7 Do not hide behind an e-mail. If an issue needs handling directly then get on the phone or visit the person.
8 Handle sensitive issues with care, it is very easy to criticize by e-mail.
9 Keep it simple. Email is good for facts but not tact or diplomacy.
10 Never argue over e-mail. Such arguments escalate too quickly. Get on the phone or visit the person to sort it out.

Real Life Application 9:

Why it's good to talk

Having a brief natter by the coffee machine has always been an essential part of daily life at work. Now though some organizations are recognizing that this type of communication is very important. Supermarket ASDA is one such organization and it is encouraging staff to get out of the habit of putting their heads down to work and not having time to chat. Staff are encouraged to take more breaks and to go into five-minute huddles before or after shifts. Formal sessions have also been set up in which managers listen to employees and, as a result of these initiatives, employee satisfaction has risen by 20 per cent.

Companies such as Heineken and Philips are tackling poor communication by selecting people who have good communication skills and who they think will get on with others. They believe that this encourages creativity and information sharing.

Article adapted from 'Why it's good to talk' by Kate Hilpern, *Guardian*, 12 April 1999.

Summary

- ASDA is encouraging more social chatting among its staff and free conversations with managers. This appears to have raised employee satisfaction.
- Other organizations are paying greater attention to selecting staff who will fit in and who have good communication skills.

Questions

1 What possible disadvantages could there be to encouraging more chatting?

2 What are the main ways of improving communication within an organization?

Essay questions

1a Describe two models of leadership. (10)

1b 'Most modern leadership models propose one style as being most effective.' Discuss.

2a Communication is often blamed for poor morale and effectiveness within an organisation. Describe the communication cycle and identify ways in which it can go wrong. (23)

3a Describe the main features of Transactional Analysis. (10)

3b How can Transactional Analysis be used to improve relationships between individuals? (13)

4 Working in groups

In the previous chapters the areas of communication, motivation and personality were covered. While most coverage was given to how they apply to the individual, this chapter looks at these topics in terms of how they apply to groups of people. In addition, the process of group formation and some of the problems associated with groups, particularly group decision making, are discussed. Real Life Applications that are considered are:

- RLA 10: Ford focuses on the value of teamwork
- RLA 11: £275 000 for woman forced to be a sumo wrestler.

Group or team?

Much of the theory in this field concerns groups. However, it is used to explain how teams can be formed and made effective. So what is the difference? For the main, the two terms can be used interchangeably particularly when talking about groups that have been formally brought together to accomplish a specific goal.

A group could simply be a number of people in close proximity, for instance a queue at a bus-stop. In most theories, however, it is assumed that there is a level of interaction and interdependency. A team would be thought of as a formal group whose members all share and work towards a common goal.

Types of groups

In a **formal** group each person has an allocated role and the objectives for each person are clearly laid down. **Informal** groups appear more spontaneously and the objective and roles become clearer over time as members of the group interact. The group can be primary or secondary. A **primary group** is small in size, with close relationships and has a lot of face to face contact. For instance a family, football team or small department. A **secondary group** is larger, more impersonal and may not even be at one location. For instance a company, a fan club or profession.

Group formation

Informal groups can form spontaneously. For instance, the line of people at a bus-stop could not really be thought of as a working group or team. If, however, the bus was late again, then they might start talking to each other and have something in common. If they decided that one of them was going

to write to the bus company and another was going to write to the papers, while the others investigated private minibus hire for that group, they would be regarded as a working group. If at the end of this process they never met again, they would be regarded as an *ad hoc* **group**. These are often formally created to complete specific projects and once the project is complete, they disband.

Whether teams are formally created or appear spontaneously, they tend to go through specific stages of formation. Tuckman (1965) identified four stages and the job and social characteristics of each one.

1 Forming

The emphasis is very much on deciding how the job is best done with the resources available. Group members tend to act cautiously with each other, not wanting to upset the team or appear too dominant. Everyone is finding out about each other. Members tend to look to the leader for guidance.

2 Storming

This is where friction starts to develop. The task and method are clear now and individuals may not like the role they need to carry out and perceive that it was not what they expected or what they should be doing. Members will now be putting forward their opinions and personalities far more, which can cause the group to become divided. This new-found independence means that they will resist the control of the leader and be interested in their own needs.

3 Norming

Concerning the task at hand, there is an open

exchange of views and feelings. There is more co-operation and a willingness to take on board the views of others. New standards (norms) for methods, values and roles are accepted by the group. The members become more of a social group who make more of an effort to avoid conflict.

4 Performing

By this stage the group have gelled together well and the task and the social aspect of the group come together, with effective interactions during task completion which is achieved by a flexible and co-operative group.

Commentary

The model suggests that any group must go through these four stages. However, there may be instances where this does not happen or simply cannot happen. For instance, in a crisis a leader may gather together a group and allocate roles. Any problems will be suppressed as everyone knows that it is not the time to express them. Equally, the model assumes that the team's membership, role and objectives remain static and this rarely happens in organizations where new people join, managers change and new projects come on board. It could be inferred that groups will rarely get beyond storming under these circumstances.

In any event the model does not give an indication of how long this process takes. Assuming that the team is small, constant and has clear objectives, the whole process could take a few months. With larger teams and more complex objectives it will probably be at least two years.

Commentary

Could the reasons for England's lack of success at football be due to the regular changes to line-up and infre-quent exposure of players to each other? Under the circumstances, the team is unlikely to get beyond storming. Also it might suffer from **role conflict**, i.e. are members England players, or do they play for their home team?

Finally, how many members of the women's England team can you name? Their lack of prominence is another example of sexual stereotyping affecting professions.

Culture

The culture of the organization will also influence groups. For instance, if a group must come up with innovative methods of producing a product, it is unlikely to succeed if the culture is one of control following existing procedures and not taking risks.

Thomsett (1980) suggested that a supportive group culture would consist of the following:

- There is a common view that people are an asset that should be developed.
- The organization should be flat with a participative management style.
- Innovation should be common and risk taking encouraged.
- Employees should have a high level of discretion.
- Groups of like-minded and skilled people are brought together.
- People's skills should match the roles they are given.

Group characteristics

Group characteristics can be organized under four main headings:

- Norms.
- Cohesiveness.
- Communication.
- Structure and dynamics.

Norms

In Chapter 2, social norms were discussed in terms of how individuals tend to take a lead from the behaviour of others and have a preference for acting in a manner acceptable to society or the group in which they exist. The bank wiring room experiment by Elton Mayo (see p. 43) where hardworkers were punished by team mates was an example of where this social norming had a negative effect. What the team was doing was maintaining its norms, in that instance the production levels were maintained by the workers, not the managers. Other negative examples appear in street cultures where gang members carry out violent acts that ordinarily they

England's football team (2000) may suffer from role conflict

would never dream of doing. It is for this reason that riot police aim to remove ring leaders from the scene as soon as possible, as other group members, free from a dominant influence may lose heart.

On a more positive note, the norms may reflect positive values such as a team spirit, helping each other, maintaining quality, seeing the customer as being more important than the team or seeing development of new skills as vital. Norms can easily vary from group to group, even if they share the same manager. It is not uncommon for one group within a company always to be regarded as negative and adversarial, even if new people join the group, as they pick up and adapt to the group norms.

Feldman (1984) identified four purposes that norms serve:

- They express the values of the group and in doing so they influence those interacting with the group.
- They simplify and make behaviour more predictable, thereby smoothing the functioning of the group.
- The norms guide the actions of group members, thus avoiding awkward situations, e.g. 'You know you don't do that around here'.
- They help the group to survive by rejecting those who do not behave as the group wishes. This deviant behaviour might be tolerated though if the deviant is influential within the group

Cohesiveness

Cohesive groups are those where sharing of ideas is promoted and they are taken on board by mutual consensus. The group will agree things among themselves and allow for both the group and the individual's needs. Such teams promote high levels of satisfaction and may actually lead to a lower turnover of staff as members do not want to leave the group.

According to McKenna (1994), factors that affect group cohesiveness include the following:

- **Similarity of attitudes and goals** between group members.
- **Time spent together**. As time passes members explore common interests and develop interpersonal attraction. A closer relationship is likely to develop if they are all physically close.
- **Isolation**. Groups isolated from other groups may consider themselves special.
- **Threats**. The group will stand together if faced by an external threat.

- **Size**. Smaller groups tend to be more cohesive whereas larger ones may split to form subgroups or cliques.
- **Stringent entry requirements**. The more difficult it is to join a group, the more cohesive it is likely to be as members will see themselves and the group as special and want to uphold that image.
- **Rewards**. Group incentive schemes may increase cohesiveness if the incentive is realistic and desirable.

There is some evidence that cohesive groups are both more satisfied and more productive. Many studies point to the team-based working systems within Japanese car factories. Some of the characteristics of the Japanese approach to teams include:

- job rotation
- the ability to stop the production line if something doesn't appear to be right (traditionally, this was a highly prized right of the supervisor)
- if one team member has a problem, it's a team problem, not an individual's problem
- if a fault is found, the team who installed that part must come to correct it
- far more decision making allowed at group level.

Studies by Hodgetts (1991) concluded that these factors result in greater effort, lower absenteeism and lower staff turnover. Others would point out that the Japanese culture places a strong emphasis on endurance, work ethic and loyalty, so the real test would be if those techniques could be replicated outside of Japan.

Commentary

Figure 4.1 shows that Japanese factories are more productive than European or US factories, even outside of Japan, where clearly the Japanese culture would not be a factor. While therefore it is easy to link team factors with productivity, Japanese factories also benefit from leading edge automation, excellent production processes, just-in-time delivery of parts, heavy emphasis on occupational health (making sure the workers are fit enough to do the job) and working to very short TAC times. A TAC time is the time allowed to complete a process. By having them very short, there is a great pressure on the worker to work fast and there is some evidence that in the UK, the most common reason for leaving a job on the production line of a Japanese factory is the inability to keep up with the pace of work.

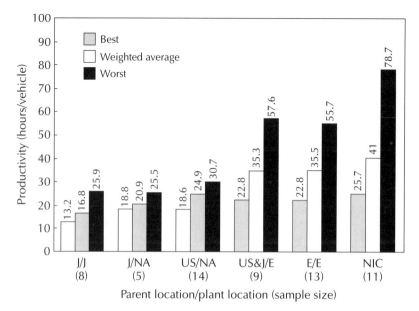

Figure 4.1: Productivity and location of factory

From M Imai *Kaizen* (1996), McGraw-Hill. Reproduced by permission.

Communication

On p. 65 communication networks were explained, in particular how some are more effective than others. Within a working group or team, communication is essential for both productivity and job satisfaction. Studies by Leavitt (1951) and Shaw (1964, see p. 64) showed that complex problems were best solved with a less centralized network such as the circle while simple ones were best solved by a more centralized network.

On p. 65 the various roles people can play in the communication process were explained. Group members may either carry out those roles as a result of their formal responsibilities or may informally develop into that role. In addition, the communication between individuals will vary between task-centred discussion and social interactions. The level of either and the manner in which it will be communicated within the team can be categorized as shown in Figure 4.2 (cited in Cowling, 1998).

Trained observers can identify these behaviours and therefore indicate the combinations of people who would best work with each other, the principle being that many of these behaviours require one of the others, e.g. number 8 and number 5. Without such combinations, communication in the group may be less effective.

If a group becomes too cohesive there can be negative effects such as abuse of power and **group think**. Teams may become so cohesive as to start to reject the control of the manager or working against the interest of the organization. There are three main ways that power is gained.

- **Co-operating.** More than one group may agree to co-operate in certain ways, such as reducing production levels, in order to force management to put on more overtime.
- **Neutralizing.** By combining with other groups, the power of another may become neutralized. Alternatively, members of another group could be invited to join on a temporary basis. By seeing that one of their own people was involved with another group's activity, there may be less resistance to it.

A. Socio-emotional: positive

1 *Shows solidarity*, raises others' status, gives help, rewards
2 *Shows tension release*, jokes, laughs, shows satisfaction
3 *Agrees*, shows passive acceptance, understands, concurs, complies

B Task: attempted answers

4 *Gives suggestion*, direction, implying autonomy for others
5 *Gives opinion*, evaluation, analysis, expresses feeling, wish
6 *Gives orientation*, information, repeats, clarifies, confirms

C Task: questions

7 *Asks for orientation*, information, repetition, confirmation
8 *Asks for opinion*, evaluation, analysis, expression of feeling
9 *Asks for suggestion*, direction, possible ways of action

D Socio-emotional: negative

10 *Disagrees*, shows passive rejection, formality, withholds help
11 *Shows tension*, asks for help, withdraws out of field
12 *Shows antagonism*, deflates others' status, defends or asserts self

Figure 4.2: Task- and social-centred interactions, based on Bales

- **Persuading.** Possibly by gaining vital information or controlling services or access to information, one group can achieve an advantage over another.

Such activities often go on either with the blessing of the group's manager, who sees a personal benefit in having a powerful team, or without the manager realizing what is happening.

Group think (Janis, 1972)

Group think is where the team strives so hard to reach a consensus on decisions that it tends to ignore other rational alternative ideas. Group pressure on individuals to conform may stifle any such suggestions, leading to a lack of creativity and risk taking. Worst of all is when the team follows an incorrect path and refuses to take on board any objections, those objections being seen as a threat which makes that team even more cohesive.

Group think can also lead to the manager losing control as the employee's loyalty and identity with the team is greater than with the manager. Janis (1972) proposes the following characteristics of group think:

- feeling of invulnerability
- feeling that the group is always right
- negative views of others
- group consensus is essential
- illusion that members of the group all have one shared opinion
- erecting a 'protective shield' around the group.

Group think may be very detrimental to an organization which may find that groups challenge management and the only course of action may be to split them up. Group think that stifles individual viewpoints can be dangerous, as seen with the US Space Shuttle *Challenger* disaster (Moorhead *et al*, 1991) where a chief engineer repeatedly raised concerns about launching when the temperature was so low. He was later found to have been put under great pressure from his colleagues to approve the launch. In another example of a tragic accident, the Chernobyl nuclear disaster in 1986 was later felt to have been influenced by the operators having a feeling of invulnerability and that any doubts people raised about procedures were censored within the group itself (Reason, 1987).

Structure and dynamics of a team

So far, a number of references have been made to the official and unofficial roles people play when in groups and the most effective communication net-

Challenger disaster – were the warnings of individuals ignored?

works. Both of these factors influence the structure of the group. Other factors include the objectives of the group, the resources available, the time frame for their objectives and the culture of the organization.

If the group is expected to be innovative then there is evidence (Meadows, 1980) that a less bureaucratic and more **flexible group structure** is preferable. To an extent the group should be allowed to do its own thing, unrestricted by rules and procedures. It should also be given a great deal of discretion and have the authority to make a wide range of decisions.

At the opposite extreme, **mechanistic structures** favour routine work where achieving a tried and tested result is required. These structures do not just apply to small groups such as a department but can apply to whole organizations. The structure of the group or organization may come about because of its culture and objectives, or the culture may develop as a result of the structure.

Charles Handy identified the following organization cultures/structures:

- **Power** – frequently found in small entrepreneurial companies. There is a central source of power with rays of power spreading out from this central figure. Control is through selecting trustworthy people.
- **Role** – very bureaucratic with many rules and procedures. They are co-ordinated from the top by a narrow band of senior managers who can control easily if everyone follows procedures.
- **Task** – a job-related culture where the right resources and people are brought together and left to get on with it. Influence is through expertise rather than formal position.
- **Person** – where individuals band together so that they can follow their own careers or projects, often sharing support staff and resources, e.g. barristers, consultants, etc.

Group roles

Within a group, a person may have a formal role and this can lead to stress and inefficiency if the individual is not clear what his or her role is (**role ambiguity**) or if the role conflicts with another (role conflict). For instance, the role of a parent and also being a busy executive (see p. 50 on stress and women).

Within a group, people display certain personality traits (see p. 56) and studies have shown that

particular combinations of traits within the team should be encouraged in order to achieve the greatest effectiveness. These combinations cause people to act in a certain unofficial role.

Meredith Belbin wrote a highly influential book *Management teams and why they succeed or fail* (1981) which included a means for identifying an individual's preferred approach to behaving within a team. The **Belbin Self Perception Inventory** (a questionnaire to identify preferred team role) has become a feature of most management courses.

Belbin identified eight roles that people tend towards (see Key Study 7). Individuals may show a

---

KEY STUDY 7

Researchers:	Meredith Belbin *et al* (1981)
Aims:	To identify the team roles necessary for effective teams.
Method:	Over nine years groups of managers were given a series of intelligence and personality tests and then put into teams in order to carry out an executive management exercise (EME) and one similar to monopoly, called teamopoly. Observers looked for the following behaviours: • asking • informing • proposing • opposing • delegating • building on ideas • commenting.
Results:	Various combinations of groups were formed, e.g. all of high intelligence (which was found to fail) or certain personality types. Extroverts performed better than introverts.
Conclusions:	That certain combinations of intelligence and personality within a group are required if optimum efficiency and group cohesiveness is to be achieved.
Critics:	Furham *et al* (1993) disputed the validity of Belbin's Self Perception Inventory and cautioned against using it as a selection tool.

preference for more than one role, in which case they may be prepared to adopt a different role if someone else displays the same preference:

- **Co-ordinator** (originally called chairperson). Calm, confident and controlled, they are adept at drawing upon the skills in the group.
- **Shaper**. A task-orientated leader, highly dynamic and driven, but often impatient and argumentative.
- **Resource investigator**. These people are able to get things done, because they 'know people'. They are creative, curious and sociable.
- **Plant**. Highly individualistic, serious minded with a strong intellect, they tend to contribute a lot to the team's performance. Often loners, they are regarded as ideas people.
- **Monitor evaluator**. Sober and unemotional, they tend to contribute only when they feel it is necessary. They are intelligent and can help to assess the arguments put forward by the plant and resource investigator.
- **Team worker or maker**. Highly people orientated, they maintain the morale and cohesiveness of the team.
- **Completer finisher**. Painstaking and orderly, they ensure that all details are checked and every aspect of a task is finished.
- **Implementor**. A practical organizer who puts the needs of the organization first. They are disciplined, tough minded and conscientious and drive the group to achieving their objectives.

Preferred combinations

Belbin suggested that the most effective teams will have one co-ordinator, plant and monitor evaluator with one or more of the other roles; in other words, a mixed team. He also suggests a number of factors that contribute to team success:

- A co-ordinator to pull the team together.
- One strong plant, producing ideas for others.
- A spread of mental abilities, one plant, another intelligent member, with a co-ordinator of above average intelligence.
- A spread in personal attributes makes for wide team role coverage and wide team role strength.
- Match between attributes and responsibilities, useful job and personal characteristics, use of pairs of team members.
- Adjustment to solve any team imbalance, i.e. the team should identify anything it is lacking and adjust accordingly.

Having completed a Belbin analysis it may be possible to select an effective group of people. However, this is probably difficult in reality.

Effective groups

While the reasons for a group being effective are complex and, as has been seen earlier, comprises a whole range of influencing factors, it is possible to differentiate between an effective team and a less effective team. McGregor (1960) summarized the differences as shown in Table 4.1.

Table 4.1: McGregor's (1960) Characteristics of effective and ineffective Groups

Effective	Ineffective
1 Informality; relaxed atmosphere; involvement; interest	Formality; tense atmosphere; indifference; boredom
2 Much discourse; high contributions	Domination by few, contributions often lack relevance
3 Understanding/acceptance of common aims	Aims ill-defined and misunderstood; conflict between private aims and common aims exists
4 Listen; consider; forward ideas	Unfair hearing; irrelevant speeches; members fear ridicule/condemnation
5 Examine disagreements; dissenters are not over-powered	Disagreements are suppressed or conflict develops; large minority is dissatisfied; disruptive minority imposes its view
6 Consensus decision making; member feels free to disagree	Lack of consensus; premature decision making; formal voting (simple majority)
7 Constructive criticism	Personalized destructive criticism
8 Feelings and attitudes are aired	Feelings remain under the surface
9 Awareness of decisions/actions; clear assignment	Lack of awareness of decisions; unclear assignments
10 Leadership role undertaken by most suitable member	Leadership role is jealously guarded
11 Frequent review of group operations	Not too concerned with deficiencies of the group

From D. McGregor *The Human Side of Enterprise.* Copyright © 1960 by McGraw-Hill, Inc. Reproduced by permission.

How groups make decisions.

Before we cover how groups make decisions, it is useful to understand how individuals do it and what types of decisions there are to be made.

Individual decision making

Most research in this area relates to deviation from rational decision making. A rational decision is one that logically should be made, however humans regularly make irrational decisions. An example would be to invest £10 in a local raffle where there was a 5000 to one chance of winning a new car or buying ten lottery tickets with a 50 million to one chance of winning £6 million. The rational decision would be to go with the higher odds, yet many would still go for the lottery. The rational decision for many teenagers is to go to university, yet the appeal of working, or travelling is very strong, albeit not necessarily rational. As for intimate personal relationships, well the choices people make are often not rational!

Arroba (1978) identified six decision making styles from a sample of managers and manual workers:

- No thought.
- Compliant – goes with what is expected to decide.
- Logical – careful consideration of all of the variables.
- Emotional – decision made on the basis of wants or likes.
- Intuitive – the decision just seems right.
- Hesitant – slow and difficult to feel committed.

Commentary

Most personality questionnaires also show people's preferences for approaching decisions. In the OPQ on p. 19, the following scales are useful: independent minded, democratic, data rational, conventional, forward thinking, trusting and decisive. The profile on p. 19 indicates that the person would probably tend to go with the consensus of the team and would not be particularly interested in analysing all of the data or checking its accuracy. The decisions would tend to focus on the short-term solution and might not be made quickly.

The value of teamwork is considered in RLA 10.

Life's decisions don't tend to be as easy to work out as the lottery odds as there are so many variables to consider. A person could evaluate alternatives using a range of important criteria or could search for an alternative that is good enough, and stop the search once it has been found, e.g. the difference between someone searching for the perfect member

Real Life Application 10:

Ford focuses on the value of teamwork

The Ford Motor Company has come up with a way of generating small ideas that it hopes will add up to the big one. It has long been recognized that in any chat between managers and other co-workers, the conversation invariably turns to how that company could be put to rights. No one knows how many brilliant ideas suggested during these chats have been lost. Day-to-day pressures means there is rarely time to refine or even remember them.

Ford plans to produce, capture and put into place any suggestion from managers that has the potential to improve the way the company does business. Staff from every division are brought together into cross-functional teams to spend three days thinking about what Ford does and how it could do it better. Everyone is encouraged to contribute. The teams mutually decide which suggestion has the most merit and then they have 90 days to implement it, with the support of senior management. Three hundred managers have been through the process and have come up with ten projects aimed at adding value to the business.

Ford has now expanded this approach worldwide and believes that it really shows that its staff are its most important asset.

Article adapted from 'Focusing on the value of teamwork' by David White, *Guardian*, 27 March 1999.

Summary

- Ford is bringing cross-functional teams together for three days to mutually agree a suggestion that could benefit the company. They then have 90 days to implement it.
- The principle is based on the idea that such conversations take place informally but no one tends to follow them up.

Questions

1 What effect could this process have on the motivation of its participants?

2 How else could such ideas be gathered?

of staff or settling for someone who is a reasonably good fit. The choice of method really depends upon what a person expects to gain from any particular method (see expectancy theory on p. 38).

Researchers have found that generally people see that a potential loss of a certain amount outweighs the potential for gaining that amount, even if the odds are the same. For instance, on the TV quiz show, *Who wants to be a millionaire?*, contestants constantly have to weigh up the possibility of doubling or halving their winnings, depending upon whether they go for the next question. On the whole, people try to avoid losing, even if the potential gains are higher.

People are also influenced by how the alternatives are put, for instance 'This operation gives you a 90 per cent chance of surviving' as opposed to 'This operation has a 10 per cent chance of you dying'. According to Kahneman and Tversky (1981), people prefer decisions with an element of risk if the stakes are high, rather than a more moderate decision with lower odds of success. For example, 'If you have this treatment there is a 90 per cent chance of success, but you could die, if it goes wrong' or 'You could have this treatment which has a 40 per cent chance of success, but you won't die if it fails'. In business this could relate to decisions that could ruin the company or guarantee its future success.

In addition to weighing up the potential gains and losses, people possess individual **heuristics**, or rules of thumb as to how they approach problems (see Table 4.2). For instance, if the head of a health authority has a budget of £1 million only and could use it either to save the lives of 50 terminally ill children or 500 terminally ill adults, which would that person choose? If redundancies need to be made, does he or she use a last-in first-out rule, even if some of the new people have young families? The individual's initial reaction would be based on a heuristic, which consists of personality, personal closeness to the decision, bias and whether someone likes to keep as many people happy as possible or go for the maximum good, for just a few people.

Group decision making

A group consists of a number of individuals, many of whom are going to come to different conclusions when faced with a decision. This could be because of their differences in experience, approach to risk, evaluation of the potential result, or in light of pressure from others. As a result, group decision making

Table 4.2: Heuristics

Deservingness	Where those who you believe are more deserving, benefit
Individual need	Where you do not look at the whole picture, e.g. the company, but look at how you can best benefit the individual
Fairness	More concerned with treating everyone fairly, i.e. everyone gains equally
Utility	Concerned with the maximum output or effect, i.e. generating the most amount of good
Ecology	Keeping all interested parties happy, particularly those who shout the loudest
Personal gain	Decisions are made so that there will be the maximum benefit to those near the decision maker

can be slow and result in a compromise, hence the saying that a camel is a horse designed by a committee!

There are though some advantages to group decision making. In particular, research shows that decisions made by groups evoke a greater level of commitment than those made by individuals (Levine and Moreland, 1990). In many instances the greater level of knowledge and experience within a group inevitably aids better decisions; take for example a quiz, anyone who has struggled to do one by themselves, will know the benefit of being in a quiz team. In that example there was a right or wrong answer, but at work things may not be so clear cut.

Brainstorming is a technique that many groups use to get to a most appropriate answer. Developed by Osborne in 1957, the technique involves all group members being given a subject or problem. They shout out any idea that comes to mind. Someone writes all of these down on a flip chart, even if they seem stupid. The reason for not evaluating them is that what might seem like a stupid statement could be someone's poor attempt at putting over something vital. Another group member might see where that person was coming from and shout out a clarification, which in turn might lead to other good ideas. After the list has been completed the group discusses each contribution and then decides which ones can be removed and the remaining ones are considered further. The method's effectiveness is put down to the fact that it mirrors how individuals bounce ideas around within the mind.

Commentary

Interestingly, research by Lamm and Trommsdorf (1973)

showed that individuals can come up with twice as many ideas as an individual in a group under the same conditions. Possible reasons include **evaluation apprehension**, where someone will not be brave enough to shout out an idea in case it is laughed at. Free riding is another possibility, i.e. where people do not bother as they know others in the group will think of loads of ideas.

Considerable research has been carried out on the differences between individual and group decisions. Volkrath *et al* (1989) found that groups recognized and could remember items they had been shown earlier better than individuals. Groups also confirm decisions, which gives individual members more confidence, e.g. if someone says, I think the answer is 100, and the others all suddenly see the logic of that answer and quickly agree, the group is more likely to decide on that answer. Sometimes, however, the person needs to prove to the others that he or she is correct and not every group member will be intelligent or specialized enough to understand the answer or the reasoning.

This effect raises the issue of status within the group. Studies by Maier and Solem (1952) found that lower status group members had less impact on decisions even if their answers were correct. They also found that even when at least one person in the group knew the correct answer, the group answer was by no means always correct (see any team quiz show for evidence of that). Lastly, while having a consensus made people feel more confident about the decision, it did not make it correct.

Subsequent work (Davis, 1982; Stasser *et al*, 1989) identified alternative criteria that a group could use to make decisions:

- **Truth wins**. If one team member knows the correct answer, then the group will recognize and follow along with it.
- **Truth supported wins**. If two people know the correct answer, the group recognizes and follows it. This is often the case with complex problems as it takes two people to say it is correct before the others believe it.
- **Majority wins**. Any decision favoured by the majority is adopted (common where there is a lack of leadership).
- **Equipotentiality**. All decisions, whether they are put forward by one or more of the group, are equally likely to be adopted.

The problem with group decision making comes when the members cannot decide between alternatives. Do they compromise or does one part of the group concede to the other? There is some evidence that rather than taking a compromise route, on the whole groups tend to take riskier decisions than was first proposed, possibly because people feel more secure making such riskier decisions, if they are not alone in making them. This is called **Group Polarization** (from one extreme to the other). Isenberg (1986) identified two main reasons why this happens. The first is **social comparison**, i.e. that people like to present themselves in a socially desirable way and therefore try to be like the other group members. The other reason is that information being discussed by the majority of the group will dominate that discussion and therefore become persuasive.

Making decisions in groups can be helped through structured decision making processes. These are only suitable for complex decisions and ones where they do not have to be made immediately. There are many such structured approaches. Here is one, used by a global manufacturing company. It consists of a series of steps, each of which employ techniques for clarifying information:

1 Describe the actual problem.
2 Identify possible causes.
3 Take short-term corrective action.
4 Gather data.
5 Conduct tests, analyse results and select solution.
6 Implement solution.
7 Evaluate solution.

Inter-group conflict

Conflict between groups can occur when:

- they have an excessive pride in their own achievements, and start disparaging others
- groups have distorted perceptions and judgements of other groups
- other groups are seen as the enemy, possibly because they are in competition with each other
- one team holds information or carries out a process that influences the success of another team.

Early studies on team rivalry were done by Sherif in 1967. His studies of groups of boys found that when split into groups they soon became hostile towards other groups (see Key Study 8).

KEY STUDY 8

Researcher:	Sherif (1967)
Aims:	To study the interaction of groups of boys.
Method:	At a boys camp, two groups were formed and deliberately arranged to encourage separate identities, i.e. two distinct groups.
Results:	The boys soon integrated within their groups and the atmosphere moved from a play-orientated to a work-like approach with an autocratic leader developing in both groups. Each group gradually began to view the other with hostility and reduced communication. In addition to the hostility, the winning group became cohesive and had a reduced need to fight. The losing group disintegrated and scapegoats were found.
Conclusions:	That identifying strongly with a group can lead to hostility towards other groups. In addition, Sherif identified reasons for conflict within the group, e.g. differences in ways things were communicated, the way work was divided up, poor motivation techniques by the leader.

Further studies of intergroup conflict have shown that it can be reduced, if:

- they are each bounded by the same rules, i.e. perceived to be in a fair situation
- resources are allocated fairly
- matrix structures are used rather than hierarchical structures (see p. 59)
- role stress is reduced
- members move between groups.

Team building.

To end this chapter on groups or teams, it is useful to look at some of the approaches used to build or improve teams. These take many varied approaches and mainly concentrate on management teams.

Typically, the team building will involve a classroom-based analysis of the team members, probably using a tool such as Belbin's Self Perception Inventory. Then the teams will be given some of the theory already discussed in this chapter. Next they will often have to break up into groups and undertake certain tasks, often outside, such as building a catapult that can fire an egg 20 feet, or removing a 'bomb' from a cordoned-off area without stepping inside that area.

Group members each take it in turns to lead the team, so that both leadership and group member skills are learned. The social bonding element of the events is often as important as the training itself.

Some team building events can go disastrously wrong. Often it is the first time that individuals have done any physical exercise for years and they can in some instances get injured or even worse have a heart attack.

Arguments can ensue, when old friction boils up when a team member lets the rest of the team down. Or in the case detailed below (see RLA 11), it can just go wrong from any angle you want to look at it!

Real Life Application 11:

£275 000 for woman forced to be a sumo wrestler

A saleswoman attended a conference and team building event organized by her employer. At only 5 ft 3 in and 8 stone, she said she did not want to participate in the team building activities which were all physical in nature. It was made clear though that it was part of the corporate culture to be a team player and that she should take part. She decided that sumo wrestling looked the least offensive event. She had to put on a heavily padded suit that made her look like a Michelin man and then she had to fight against an opponent. Within minutes she had bounced off her opponent and banged her head, rendering her unconscious. As a result, she has developed epilepsy and is unable to drive. A judge awarded her £275,000 in compensation.

Article adapted from '£¼ million for a woman forced to be a sumo wrestler', *Daily Mail*, 10 May 2000.

Summary

- A sales company organized a team building event with a variety of physical activities and everyone was expected to participate. As a result one employee was injured.

Questions

1 To what extent do you think such activities actually build teams?

2 What alternatives could the company have used?

Essay questions

1 Discuss, using examples, Tuckman's theory of group formation. (23)

2 'Working in teams is far more effective than the traditional method of working as individuals.' Discuss.

3a Meredith Belbin identified key roles within an effective team. Describe these roles. (10)

3b Discuss the effects on a team of two different combinations of 'Belbin team members.'

A Advice on answering essay questions

Chapter 1

1a Their standardization, validity, reliability and the norm group with which you are comparing the results. Good answers should give examples of appropriate and inappropriate tests for particular jobs and explain reliability, validity and standardization.

1b 'Discuss' generally means 'arguments for and against'. So in this instance why tests are controversial (are they testing the right things, are they valid, reliable and used properly? Do they discriminate against certain ethnic groups?) and why much of this controversy is unfounded (tests from renowned companies are well constructed, those using them must be trained, validity studies show their effectiveness).

2a Try to be able to draw the table on p. 17 and be able to explain it.

2b Better question design; not using clinical tests and making them more occupationally based; better training for testers.

3 Explain what EI is and mention Daniel Goleman's book. While Goleman favours its use, there is little valid evidence for EI so other selection methods could be said to be more effective. Mention that EI tends to be looked at in personality questionnaires anyway, so is it necessary to separate it out?

Chapter 2

1 Briefly set the meaning of work in context, possibly with some historical or cross-cultural information (but not too much as the question is about the psychological theories). We work partly out of need for resources such as food but also due to conformity, obedience, normative social influence and social facilitation. Good answers will link this to motivation theory such as Maslow's hierarchy of needs.

2a Extrinsic motivators are those outside of the job itself such as money, perks, working conditions and holidays. Herzberg called them hygiene factors because if you disinfect an operating theatre you may stop people getting ill, but not doing it will not make people healthy. Similarly improving office conditions will not motivate people more. However, move people to a shabby, cold office and it will demotivate them.

2b It is always good to back up any answer with a real life example even if it is not asked for. Study the RLA's in Chapter 2. You should also ask friends and family for examples in their work and remember them for your exam. Make sure you do not confuse extrinsic and intrinsic when giving examples.

3a Shift working, long hours, physical hardship, poor conditions, dealing with the public, having little control over work methods and outcome. Particularly stressful jobs include teaching, production line working and nursing. Women and minority groups face additional pressures.

3b Irritability, mood swings, headaches, poor skin condition, upset stomach leading to increased absence, mistakes and accidents. Stress can lead to heart disease and cancer. Excellent answers will explain the dual response system and get the spelling of words like norepinephrine correct!

Chapter 3

1a Describe (as opposed to discuss) two models such as the managerial grid, Adair's model or Lewin's scale. Try to learn ones that can be explained using a diagram and where you can relate this to examples.

1b Participative approaches i.e. getting employees involved and giving them responsibility are advocated by various models. However goal setting theory is too. Situational leadership theories advocate changing your style as appropriate. Your answer should show that you understand some of the most recognised techniques and that there isn't just one right way of managing.

2   Learn the communication cycle diagram (p. 63). It can go wrong at any point however 'noise' is the main cause (give examples).

3   TA (Berne and Harris) revolves around communicators being in one of three possible states, Adult, Parent or Child. Each requires to be treated in a certain way, not doing so causes crossed transactions. Show the possible transactions as a diagram (always refer to any diagram you draw, in your answer do not just expect the examiner to know why you have put it there).

3b The questioner wants to know how TA can be used to improve communication so be careful not to go into detail about this in 3a. By better understanding the various transactions and training people to adapt the way they interact, communication can improve.

Chapter 4

1a Think of an example, such as a new accounts or football team and go through the stages of forming, storming, norming and performing.

2   Explain why groups might be more effective (better decisions, social facilitation, mutual support) and why they might not (group think, poor team structure, competition between teams).

3a See p. 77 for the names and descriptions, it is worth remembering these. This might be easier if you do the self-perception questionnaire yourself. It is in Belbin's book *Management teams and why they succeed or fail* which can be found in most libraries.

3b Discuss Belbin's recommended mixture of roles (p. 77) and one where there is a Chairperson and a Shaper, but that is missing other key roles. This should give you plenty to write about and contrast nicely with the ideal structure.

A Advice on answering short answer questions

Chapter 1

RLA 1

1 IQ is measuring intelligence yet there are various theories about what intelligence actually is. IQ doesn't always reflect intelligence (Ceci 1996) and tests seem to show that IQ is rising over time, yet this is unlikely to be true.

2 The environment in which she was brought up, or that her real father was very intelligent or of course it could be that the Mensa test result doesn't actually reflect her true intelligence.

RLA 2

1 Remember correlation does not mean cause. Those people who went on the EI course could already be the better sales people or be those who respond best to the challenge of increasing their sales. Course participants may have been given encouragement that others did not receive.

2 Any job that involves direct contact with people, e.g. customer service, telesales, nursing.

Figure 1.26

The top distribution curve may be showing that the majority of employees do not perform well or the assessment was done by a 'hard marker'. The opposite situation applies in the other curve.

Chapter 2

RLA 3

1 Clearly managers should ensure that causes of frustration, e.g. lack of basic resources, are solved. Focus groups could be run to find out more reasons at a local level. If more money cannot be awarded then flexible hours and benefits may help.

2 These actions would show nurses' problems are regarded as important. Flexible working hours and benefits may lead to greater staff retention, particularly when nurses have children of their own.

RLA 4

1 The factors for why the British are less satisfied may not be as pronounced elsewhere, or possibly leadership styles are different in other countries leading to a more positive outlook. Also there is evidence from marketing researchers that people from Southern Europe respond more positively to **any** survey than the British, so possibly the results are distorted.

2 The sample size per country, the demographic profile (age, sex etc.) of the sample. The questioning technique, how were the questions translated, were there any major recent events in that country that may have led to a particularly positive or negative feeling.

RLA 5

1 They might feel that employees with children are being treated better (equity theory) or that the money spent on those initiatives could have been in their salaries.

2 Those companies may have more effective systems and procedures and have selected more efficient employees.

3 Equity theory, Maslow's 'security' needs.

Chapter 3

RLA 6

1 The survey results are about people's perceptions as opposed to actual data such as the number of employees arriving late, dismissed for sexual harassment etc. The results are therefore subjective.

2 Dressing smartly may give others an impression of authority or status, hence police, judges and

medical consultants dressing formally. Would you have more confidence in a solicitor who wore a suit, than one who wore shorts and a T-shirt? Dressing casually, though, could make people feel more relaxed e.g. judges not wearing wigs and gowns in child cases.

3   Extrinsic because it is not part of the job itself.

RLA 7

1   Because employees are owners of the company and therefore must receive consistent information and have an effective method of voicing their views to senior management.

2   Intranet, suggestion schemes, notice boards, all information going via line managers.

3   Increased motivation, better decision making, less rumours.

RLA 8

1   We are singing from the same hymn sheet; let's band together.
    He will not play ball; three strikes and you are out.

RLA 9

1   Less work might get done, rumours may spread and not everyone is as social as others.

2   Ensuring that messages are clear concise and

timely, managers are trained in communication skills, verbal information is backed up by written notices/magazines and everybody receives information relevant to them. Information overload should be avoided, i.e. people do not need to know everything.

Chapter 4

RLA 10

1   It could improve motivation as people feel their ideas are important. It could however frustrate those who feel their ideas were ignored or stolen.

2   A postal suggestion scheme with a bonus payment if the idea is taken up. Improvement teams consisting of people from all levels and functions could concentrate on solving particular problems. Managers could do a better job of listening to and acting upon suggestions.

RLA 11

1   Views vary but there is little evidence that they affect teams, in fact by adding a competitive element they may split teams. They are generally just good fun (for most people) and a welcome break from the pressures of work.

2   Better selection of team members, improved communication methods, team bonuses or getting the teams to organize the event.

R Selected references

Adair, J (1989) *Action Centred Leader*. London: The Industrial Society.

Adams, JS (1963) 'Towards an understanding of inequity.' *Journal of Abnormal and Social Psychology*, Vol. II.

Aldefer, C (1972) *Existence, relatedness and growth*. New York: Free Press.

Arnold, J, Robertson, I and Cooper, C (1991) *Work psychology*. London: Pitman.

Arroba, TY (1978) 'Decision making style of an occupational group.' *Journal of occupational psychology*, 51, pp. 219–26.

Asch, S (1955) 'Opinion and social pressure.' *Scientific American*,193, pp. 31–5.

Ash, R A and Levine, EL (1980) 'A framework for evaluating job analysis methods.' *Personnel*, 57(6), pp. 53–9.

Asher, JJ (1972) 'The biographical item, can it be improved?' *Personnel psychology*, 25, pp. 251–69.

Austin, J and Bobko, P (1985) 'Goal setting theory; unexplored areas and future research needs.' *Journal of occupational psychology*, 58, pp. 289–308.

Behling, O (1998) 'Employee selection: will intelligence and conscientiousness do the job?' *Academy of management executives*, 12(1), pp. 77–87.

Belbin, M (1981) *Management teams: why they succeed or fail*. Oxford: Heinemann.

Betts, PW (1993) *Supervisory management*. London: Pitman.

Blake, R and Mouton, JS (1985) *The managerial grid III*. Houston, TX: Gulf Publishing.

Boring, E (1923) In E Boring (1967) *History of psychology*. Worcester MA: Clark University Press.

Browning, C (1992) *Ordinary men, reserve police battalion 101*. New York: HarperCollins.

Byham, B (1991) *Zapp*. London: Business Books.

Calvin, W (1998) 'The emergence of intelligence.' from American Scientist Internet Service, November (1998).

Cassidy, T and Lynn, R (1989) 'A multifactoral approach to achievement motivation.' *Journal of occupational psychology*, 62, pp. 310–12.

Ceci, S and Liker, J (1986) 'A day at the races: a study of IQ expertise and cognitive complexity.' *Journal of experimental psychology*, 115, pp. 225–66.

Cohen, S, Kaplan, JR, Cunnick, JE, Manuck, SB and Rabin, BS (1992) 'Chronic social stress, affiliation and cellular immune response in non human primates.' *Psychological science*, 3, pp. 301–4.

Collins, D (1994) 'The disempowering logic of empowerment.' *Empowerment in organizations*, 2(2), MCB University Press.

Cooper, CJ, Cooper, RD and Eaker, LH (1998) *Living with stress*. Harmondsworth: Penguin.

Covey, S (1989) *Seven habits of highly effective people*. North Province, Utah: Franklin Covey.

Curtis, J and Detert, R (1981) *How to relax*. Mountain View, CA: Mayfield Publishing.

Davis, K (1976) 'Understanding the organizational grapevine.' *Business and public affairs*, no. 5.

De Nisi, AS and Mitchell, J (1978) 'An analysis of peer ratings.' *Academy of management review*, 3, pp. 369–74.

DuBrin, AJ (1990) *Effective business psychology*, (3rd edn), New Jersey: Prentice Hall.

Errez, M (1977) 'Feedback, a necessary condition.' *Journal of applied psychology*, 62, pp. 624–7.

Esses, VM and Webster, CD (1988) 'Physical attractiveness, dangerousness, and the Canadian criminal code.' *Journal of applied social psychology*, 18, pp. 1017–31.

Fiedler, FE (1967) *A theory of leadership effectiveness*. New York: McGraw Hill.

Flannagan, JJ (1954) 'The critical incident technique.' *Psychological bulletin*, 51, pp, 327–58.

Fleishman, EA and Harris, EF (1962) 'Patterns of leadership behaviour.' *Personnel psychology*, 15, pp. 43–56.

Flyn, JR (1987) 'Massive IQ gains in 14 nations. What IQ really measures.' *Psychological bulletin*, 107, pp. 171–91.

Fredman, M and Ulmer, D (1984) *Treating Type A behaviour and your heart*. New York: Knopf.

Fryer, D and Payne, R (1986) 'Being unemployed.' In E McKenna (1994) *Business psychology and organizational behaviour*. Hove: Lawrence Erlbaum.

Gardner, H (1983) *Frames of mind: the theory of multiple intelligencies*. New York: Basic Books.

Ghiselli, E and Brown, C (1955). In O Behling (1998) 'Employee selection: will intelligence and conscientiousness do the job?'. *Academy of Management Executives*, 12(1), pp. 77–87.

Gillespie, R (1991) *Manufacturing knowledge, a history of the Hawthorne experiments*. Cambridge: Cambridge University Press.

Goldberg, LR and Grenier, JM (1991) *Questionnaires used in the prediction of trustworthiness in pre employment selection decisions*. Washington, DC: American Psychological Society.

Goldthorpe, J and Lockwood, D (1968) *The affluent worker, industrial attitudes and behaviour*. Cambridge: Cambridge University Press.

Goleman, D (1995) *Emotional intelligence*. New York: Bantam.

Graham, H and Bennet, R (1974) *Human resource management*. London: Pitman.

Guilford, JP (1967) *The nature of human intelligence*. New York: McGraw Hill.

Hackman, JR and Oldham, GR (1975) 'A new stage for job enrichment.' *California management review*, 17, pp. 57–71.

Hall, DT and Goodale, JG (1986) *Human resource management*. Washington, DC: Glenview, Scott, Foresman.

Handy, C (1993) *Understanding organizations*. Harmondsworth: Penguin.

Hernstein, R and Murray, C (1994) *The bell curve*. New York: Free Press.

Herzberg, F (1968) 'How do you motivate employees?' *Harvard Business Review*, January/February, pp. 53–62.

Hodgetts, R (1991) *Organizational behaviour, theory and practice*. New York: Macmillan.

Hogan, R (1990) *Hogan personality inventory manual*. Minneapolis: National Computer Systems.

Horn, J and Loehlin, J (1979) 'Intellectual resemblance among adoptive and biological relatives.' *Behaviour Genetics*, 9, pp.177–208.

Horn, J (1983) 'Texas adoption project.' *Child development*, 54, pp. 268–75.

Imai, M (1986) *Kaizen*. New York: McGraw-Hill.

Isenberg, D (1986) 'Group polarisation. A critical review and meta analysis.' *Journal of personal and social psychology*, 50, pp. 1141–51.

Jahoda, M (1979) 'The impact of unemployment in the 1930s and 1970s.' *Bulletin of British Psychological Society,* 32, pp. 309–14.

Janis, I (1972) *Group think*. Boston, MA: Houghton Mifflin.

Kahneman, D and Tversky, A (1981) *The framing of decisions and the psychology of choice*. New York: Cambridge University Press.

Kanter, RM (1979) *Change masters*. New York: Simon and Schuster.

Kelly, GA (1955) *The psychology of personal constructs*. New York: WW Norton.

Klein, HJ (1989) 'An integrated control theory model of work motivation.' *Academy of managerial review,* 14, 150–172.

Kleitman, N (1963) In P Warr (ed.) (1971) *Psychology at work*, p. 21. Harmondsworth: Penguin.

Kohn, A (1993) 'Why incentive plans cannot work.' *Harvard business review*, September.

Lamm, H and Trommsdorff, G (1973) 'Group versus individual performance.' *European journal of social psychology*, 3, pp. 361–87.

Lashley, J and McGoldrick, J (1994) *The limits of empowerment in organizations*, 2 (3) pp. 25–38. MCB University Press.

Lawler, EE (1981) *Pay and organization development*. Reading, MA: Addison Wesley.

Leavitt, HJ (1951) 'Some effects of certain communication patters on group performance.' *Journal of abnormal and social psychology*, 46, pp. 38–50.

Lewin, K (1958) 'Group decision making and social change.' In E McKenna (1994) *Business psychology and organizational behaviour*. Hove: Lawrence Erlbaum.

Locke, EA, Shaw, KN, Saari, LM and Latham,GP (1981) 'Goal setting and task performance 1969–1980.' *Psychological bulletin*, 90, pp. 125–52.

Maier, N and Solem, A (1952) 'The contribution of a discussion leader to the quality of group thinking.' *Human relations,* 5, pp. 277–88.

Marchington, M (1995) 'Fairy tales and magic wands.' *Employee relations*, 17(1), pp. 51–6. MCB University Press.

Maslow, AH (1970) *Motivation and personality*. New York: Harper & Row.

McAffee, B, Quarstein, V and Adralan, A (1995) 'The effect of discretion, outcome feedback and process feedback on employee job satisfaction in industrial management and data systems.' *Motivation and Personality*, 95, pp. 7–12.

McClelland, D (1991) *The achieving society*. Princetown, NJ: Van Nostrand.

McCormick, EJ, Jeaneret, P and Meacham, R (1972) 'A study of job characteristics and job dimensions.' *Journal of applied psychology*, 36, pp. 347–68.

McDermott, I and O'Connor J (1997) *Practical NLP for managers*. Aldershot: Gower.

McGregor, D (1960) *The human side of enterprise.* New York: McGraw-Hill.

McKenna, E (1994) *Business psychology and organizational behaviour.* Hove: Lawrence Erlbaum.

Mento, AJ, Steel, RP and Karren, RJ (1987) 'A meta analytical study of the effects of goal setting on task performance, 1966–1984.' *Organizational behaviour and human decision processes*, 39, pp. 52–83.

Milgram, S (1974) *Obedience to authority.* New York: Harper & Row.

Moorhead, G and Griffen, RW (1992) *Organizational behaviour.* 3rd edn. Boston, MA: Houghton Mifflin.

Morgan, G (1998) *Images of organization.* London: Sage.

Nisbett, RE and Wilson, T D (1977) 'The halo effect: Evidence for unconscious alteration of judgments.' *Journal of personality and social psychology*, 35, pp. 250–56.

Pease, A (1981) *Body language.* London: Sheldon Press.

Pfeffer, J (1998) 'Six dangerous myths about pay.' *Harvard business review*, May/June.

Phares, EJ (1997) *Introduction to personality.* Reading, MA: Addison Wesley.

Phillips, AP and Dipboye, RL (1989) 'Correlational tests of prediction from a process model of the interview.' *Journal of applied psychology*, February, pp. 41–52.

Porter, L and Lawler, E (1968) *Managerial attitudes and performance.* Homewood, IL: RD Irwin.

Roberts, K (1975) 'The developmental theory of occupational choice.' In T Watson (1987) *Sociology work and industry.* London: Routledge.

Robbins, SP (1991) *Organizational behaviour, concepts, controversies and applications.* New York: Prentice Hall.

Robinson, S and Rousseau, D (1994) 'Violating the psychological contract, not the exception but the norm.' *Journal of organizational behaviour,* 15, pp. 245–59.

Rutenfranz, J (1970) In P Warr (ed.) (1971) *Psychology at work*, p. 21. Harmondsworth: Penguin.

Schein, E (1978) *Career dynamics.* Reading, MA: Addison Wesley.

Schein, E (1990) 'Organizational Culture.' *American psychologist*, February, 45(2), pp. 109–19.

Schmidt, F and Hunter, J (1992) In O Behling (1998) 'Employee selection: will intelligence and conscientiousness do the job?' *Academy of management executives*, 12(1), pp. 77–87.

Schuler, R (1977) 'Role perception, satisfaction and performance moderated by organizational level and participation in decision making.' *Academy of management journal,* 120(1), pp. 159–65.

Selye, H (1976) *The stress of life.* New York: McGraw-Hill.

Shaw, ME (1964) *Communication networks in advances in experimental social psychology.* Vol.1. Academic Press.

Sherif, M (1967) *Group conflict and co-operation.* London: Routledge.

Sigman, A (1993) 'Working shifts on the red eye.' *Personnel manager plus*, October, p.19.

Smith, CS and Branick, MT (1993) 'A role and expectancy model of participative decision making.' *Journal of organizational behaviour,* 112, p. 23.

Spearman, C (1923) *The nature of intelligence and principal of cognition.* London: Macmillan.

Sternberg, RJ and Salter,W (1982) 'Conceptions of intelligence.' In RJ Sternberg, *Handbook of human intelligence*, New York: Cambridge University Press.

Thomsett, R (1980) *People and project management.* New York: Yourdon Press.

Thurstone, L (1938) 'Primary mental abilities.' *Psychometric Monographs*, no. 1.

Towler, G (1986) 'From zero to one hundred: coaction in a natural setting.' *Perception and motor skills*, 62, pp. 377–8.

Triandes, H (1994) *Culture and social behaviour.* New York: McGraw-Hill.

Triplett, N (1898) 'The dynamogenic factors in pacemaking.' *American journal of psychology*, 9, pp. 507–33.

Truckman, BW (1965) 'Development sequence of smaller groups.' *Psychological bulletin*, 63, pp. 384–99.

Vernon, PE (1950) 'The hierarchy of ability.' In *Intelligence and Ability.* Harmondsworth: Penguin.

Vollrath, D and Sheppard, BH (1989) 'Memory performance by decision making groups and individuals.' *Organization behaviour and human decision processes*, 44, pp. 289–300.

Vroom, VH (1964) *Work and Motivation.* Chichester: Wiley.

Warr, PB and Jackson, PR (1984) 'Men without jobs: some correlates of age and length of unemployment.' *Journal of occupational psychology*, 57, pp. 77–85.

Watson, T (1987) *Sociology work and industry.* London: Routledge.

Watson, T (1994) *In search of management*. London: Routledge.

Welner, A, Marten, S, Wochnick, E, Davis, M, Fishman, R and Clayton, J (1979) 'Psychiatric disorders among professional women.' *Archives of general psychiatry*, 36, pp. 169–73.

Wicks, RP (1984) 'Interviewing practical aspects.' In E McKenna (1994) *Business psychology and organizational behaviour*. Hove: Lawrence Erlbaum.

Wilkinson, H (1999) 'Honey I'm still home.' *Guardian*, 14 July.

Woodworth, RS (1928) www.psychcorp.com/sub/whoweare/wwarsw.htm

Yetton, PW (1984) 'Leadership and supervision.' In J Arnold, I Robertson and C Cooper (1991) *Work psychology*. London: Pitman.

Zaremba, A (1988) 'Working with the organizational grapevine.' *Personnel journal*, July, pp. 38–42.

Zohar, D (2000) www.mastersforum.com/zohar/zohar.txt

Saville and Holdsworth www.shlgroup.com/

DDI www.ddiworld.com/about/biobyham.asp

British Psychological Society (BPS) www.bps.org.uk/index.cfm

Ⓘ Index